THE
CLIFF ATKINSON
BACKCHANNEL

How Audiences Are Using Twitter and Social Media and Changing Presentations Forever

New
Riders

VOICES THAT MATTER™

**The Backchannel: How Audiences Are Using Twitter
and Social Media and Changing Presentations Forever**
Cliff Atkinson

New Riders
1249 Eighth Street
Berkeley, CA 94710
510/524-2178
510/524-2221 (fax)

Find us on the Web at: www.newriders.com
To report errors, please send a note to errata@peachpit.com

New Riders is an imprint of Peachpit, a division of Pearson Education

Copyright © 2010 by Cliff Atkinson

Project Editor: Michael J. Nolan
Development Editor: Box Twelve Communications, Inc.
Production Editor: Hilal Sala
Copyeditor: Darren Meiss
Proofreader: Doug Adrianson
Indexer: Fred Liese
Design Direction: Charlene Charles-Will
Cover Design: Terri Bogaards
Cover and Interior Illustrations: John Weber
Interior Design: Kathleen Cunningham
Compositor: David Van Ness

ISBN 13: 978-0-321-65951-4
ISBN 10: 0-321-65951-1

9 8 7 6 5 4 3 2 1

Printed and bound in the United States of America

To Matt Fox

Contents

Introduction x

[1] Why Are You Calling Me a #@*% on Twitter?   1

A Whole New Audience   3

The Seeds of Conflict   9

Introducing the Backchannel 16

Back from the Brink 19

A New View from the Podium 24

[2] How to Join a Twitter Backchannel . . . 29

The Backchannel and the Rise of Twitter 30

Choosing Twitter as a Backchannel Tool 33

Step 1: Open Up a Twitter Account 36

Step 2: Preview a Backchannel Twitterstream . . . 40

Step 3: Begin Growing a Twitter Community . . . 44

The Rewards and Risks of the Backchannel 47

[3] The Rewards of the Backchannel 49

A Cure for Hiccups, or a Presentation Revolution? . 50

How a Backchannel Changes Presentations   . . . 51

The Reward of Engaging Information More Fully . . 57

The Reward of Engaging One Another 59

The Reward of More Feedback 62

The Reward of Reading the Minds of Audiences . . 63

Diving In to the Backchannel Controversies 65

[4] The Risks of the Backchannel 67

The Keyboard vs. the Microphone 68

The Risk of Incivility 68

The Risk of Distraction and Confusion 71

The Risk of Unfairness 72

The Risk of Chaos 74

Understanding Backchannel Blowups 76

Audiences Are Changing in Fundamental Ways . . 76

Opening Up to Change in Presentation Approaches 80

Maximizing the Rewards, Minimizing the Risks . . 85

[5] Preparing for the Backchannel 89

Affirming What Doesn't Change 90

Surveying the New Landscape of the Backchannel . 91

Starting an Even Bigger Conversation 94

Creating a Presentation Home Page 99

Setting Up a Presentation Wiki as a Simple Start . 101

Adding More Material to Your Presentation

    Home Page 103

Facilitating a Backchannel in the Room 108

Working with the Host on the Fundamentals . . . 111

Getting Ready To Get Your Content Ready 113

[6] Making Your Ideas Twitter-Friendly . . . 115

Becoming a Filter for Your Audiences 116

Defining Your Most Important Points 118

The Rule of Four Tweets 120

Breaking Up Your Ideas into Twitter-sized Chunks . 121

Putting Your Four Tweets in the Context of a Story . 124

Beginning the Process of Distilling Your Ideas . . . 126

Writing Your Four Tweets on Four Slides 134

Building Sections Around Your Tweets 140

Preparing Your Slides for Camera Phones

    and Handheld Video Cameras 141

Getting Ready To Start the Conversation 143

[7] Joining the Backchannel in Conversation . 145

Creating a Hybrid of Presentation
and Conversation 146

Adjusting to a More Conversational Presentation . 149

Starting the Backchannel Conversation Early . . . 151

Setting Up for the Backchannel 154

Welcoming the Backchannel as You Begin 156

Starting Strong 158

Taking at Least Three Twitter breaks 161

Automating Your Involvement in the Backchannel . 165

Involving Your Audience Using Twitter
and the Web 166

Focusing the Attention of the Backchannel 168

Wrapping Up 172

Checking Your Results in the Twitterstream 173

Continuing the Backchannel Conversation 174

[8] Handling Instant Feedback from
the Backchannel 177

The Power of Negative Backchannel Feedback . . 178

Neutralizing Negativity and Snowballing Positivity . 179

Preparing Yourself for Negative
Backchannel Feedback 181

Should You Ignore or Call Out
Negative Comments? 182

Practicing Backchannel Feedback Scenarios . . . 186

Keeping the Presentation on Track 190

[9]   Holding Together the Backchannel
Experience   193
Turning Around an Unruly Backchannel   194
Establish a Reputation   198
Listen and Collect Stories   199
Dispense with Pretense   200
Talk to the Elephant in the Room (If There Is One) .   200
Make It You, You, You Instead of Me, Me, Me . . .   201
Check In with the Audience Early and Often   202
Improvise   203
Stay Grounded   205
Ignore the Small Stuff   206
Keep Things in Perspective   206
Backchannel to the Future   207

Appendix A: The Four Tweets Worksheet   210
Appendix B: The Ten Tweets Worksheet   211
Index   213

Bonus content at www.backchannelbook.com:

Web Appendix C: Negotiating a Backchannel Agreement

Web Appendix D: How Open Space Transforms Meetings

Acknowledgements

Thanks to...

Jared Goralnick, who persuaded me to join him at a panel discussion at the South by Southwest Interactive Festival in Austin in 2009, and...

Dave Gray, who welcomed me to the world of Twitter while I was there, and...

Hugh Forrest and the team at SXSW, for creating a hotbed of social innovation where I could experience the backchannel for myself, and...

Michael Nolan, who happened to be at SXSW and asked me if I had anything interesting I wanted to write about, and...

New Riders for approving my book proposal in a week and publishing my book in months, and...

Jeff Riley for masterful editing, Charlene Will for creative designing, and Hilal Sala for efficient producing, and the rest of the New Riders team for your help...

Olivia Mitchell and Tony Ramos for reviewing the first draft and offering insightful advice, and...

Chris Brogan, Brad Templeton, Craig Ball, Bert Decker, Todd Satterstein, Jaine Fraser, Jen McClure, Jared Spool, David Meerman Scott, Hugh Forrest, Nancy White, Brian Ott, Karen Lawson, Dan Gillmor, Pam Slim, Whitney Hess, Guy Kawasaki, Harrison Owen, Lisa Heft, Kaliya Hamlin, and Donella Evoniuk for graciously offering time for their background interviews, and...

The thousands of people in the backchannel who are pioneering new relationships between audiences and presenters and setting the stage for a much more conversational and effective way of communication; and...

Andrew and my extended family, including Reuben, Hilda, Reuben Jr., Vicki, Steve, and Barb.

About the Author

Cliff Atkinson is an acclaimed writer, popular keynote speaker, and an independent consultant to leading attorneys and Fortune 500 companies. He designed the presentations that helped persuade a jury to award a $253 million verdict to the plaintiff in the nation's first Vioxx trial in 2005, presentations which *Fortune* magazine called "frighteningly powerful."

Cliff's best-selling book *Beyond Bullet Points* (Microsoft Press, 2007) was named a Best Book of 2007 by the editors of Amazon.com, and it expands on a communications approach he has taught at many of the country's top law firms, government agencies, business schools, and corporations, including Sony, Toyota, Nestlé, Nokia, Nationwide, Deloitte, Amgen, Bristol-Myers Squibb, Intel, Microsoft, and the United Nations International Criminal Tribunal.

Introduction

Back in the good old days of presentations, a speaker could count on audience members to sit quietly in their chairs until they were given permission to ask questions.

Those days are rapidly drawing to a close.

More and more audience members are now bringing their laptops and smartphones into meeting rooms and using them to connect with one another and start their own conversations—while the presenter is speaking.

Sometimes these conversations are confined only to the audience members attending the presentation. But when audiences use a microblogging tool called Twitter, everything they say is published instantly and available for the world to see.

This new conversation that audiences create during a presentation is called a *backchannel*—and like any change, the backchannel can be a double-edged sword.

On one side, when audiences find a presentation interesting and useful, they use the backchannel to enhance the information they are hearing and to broadcast good ideas to people both inside and outside the room. When presenters learn about the backchannel and tap into its potential, they find it a valuable way to know their audiences better, and to find out what's really on their minds.

On the other side, when audiences find a presentation boring, not relevant, or out of date, they don't hesitate to speak their minds and publish their comments to the world. When presenters aren't aware of the backchannel or read critical comments from audience members, it can lead to public conflict that disrupts or even derails presentations.

Whichever way the sword swings, there's no doubt the backchannel is here to stay, and that it will change presentations forever. The only question is the degree of change and how meeting organizers, audience members, and presenters will address it.

The backchannel is such a new phenomenon that this book can only be a first glimpse of the new forces it introduces, and a preview of practical steps you can take to engage the new world of presentations it is creating.

Chapter 1 tells the story of the impact the backchannel can have on a presentation, and the new dynamics it introduces.

Chapter 2 explains how you can join a Twitter backchannel, and Chapters 3 and 4 describe the rewards and risks of doing so.

Chapter 5 explains what you can do to start getting ready for a backchannel, Chapter 6 helps you make your ideas more Twitter-friendly, and Chapter 7 offers specific things you can do to engage the backchannel in conversation.

Chapter 8 takes you through some scenarios so you can practice getting real-time feedback from the backchannel, and Chapter 9 describes how you can learn from the example of people who handle the backchannel well.

Appendixes A and B show a couple of helpful worksheets—the Four Tweets worksheet and the Ten Tweets worksheet—that help you condense and organize your presentation tweets.

As bonus content, go to www.backchannelbook.com to download Web Appendixes C and D. Web Appendix C presents the draft of a backchannel agreement that offers a way for presenters and audiences to negotiate the major changes at work today. And Web Appendix D covers the Open Space movement, which is changing the larger context for presentations and the backchannel today.

Together the chapters provide a first look into something very big on the horizon that is rapidly heading your way.

Nobody has the answers to the questions the backchannel presents, nor are there any ground rules to guide us.

Together we get to make the rules as we go along, in a spirit of creating effective communication experiences for anyone who gathers for a presentation.

You already live in the world of the backchannel.

What this world becomes is in your hands.

Why Are You Calling Me a #@*% on Twitter?

A speaker confronts an audience member over
a Twitter post, demonstrating the new dynamics
at work when a backchannel exists in a room

P am Slim was nervous. Sure, everybody gets anxious when they're going to speak in public, as she was scheduled to do that afternoon. But this feeling was different. She had heard that audiences at her event did not always sit quietly and passively in their seats, and that anything could happen. It would soon turn out that Pam was right to be worried.

Pam crossed Congress Avenue and headed to the Austin Convention Center, a sprawling complex covering six downtown city blocks in this thriving city of 750,000. For five days in the spring, the South by Southwest Interactive Festival here draws technologists, entrepreneurs, artists, businesspeople, and experts shaping web technology trends and culture.

(Photo and sketch courtesy of Mike Rohde)

Someone especially excited to attend Pam's session rushed to Room 18 at the far end of the convention center. Whitney Hess had flown to Austin from New York, where she is a *user experience designer*—someone who specializes in making websites and products easier to use. Whitney has her own weblog, or blog, where she publishes articles and interviews related to her profession and her life.

As one of the first to arrive, Whitney was glad to find a seat at the center of the action—first row, next to the center aisle. She sat down in her chair, pulled out her MacBook, and made sure her wireless connection was working properly. Whitney wasn't the only one using a laptop—as more people filtered into the room as she waited the 10 minutes for the panel to start, many of them started setting up their own equipment.

What made Whitney different from attendees at most other events was that she planned to use a service called Twitter that gives her the ability to instantly publish brief posts to the web. While Whitney uses her regular blog to publish posts of any size including text, images, and video, she uses Twitter to publish posts limited to 140 characters of text—around the size of a text message on a mobile phone. A post on Twitter is also called a *tweet*; the act of posting is often called *tweeting* or *Twittering*.

Whitney typed her first post on her computer and clicked to publish it (**Figure 1-1**).

I'm live-Twittering "From Blog to Book Deal" with @gapingvoid @guykawasaki @stephanieklein @katelaurielee @pamslim http://is.gd/nM4E #sxswi

Twitter text posts are so constrained in size they demand a certain writing style that gets to the point quickly in as few characters as possible. Though Whitney's post was brief, it revealed a great deal of information—not only about her intended message, but also about the sea change that many audiences and presenters are on the verge of experiencing today.

> **tip ❯** If you don't have a Twitter account, setting one up is fast and easy—you'll learn how in Chapter 2.

It is only by breaking down Whitney's tweet into its parts that you can begin to translate the shorthand she was using.

A Whole New Audience

Millions of people use Twitter in an astonishing variety of ways, well beyond what its inventors envisioned for it when it first entered the scene in 2006. Some people use Twitter to post updates on what they are doing or thinking at the moment—similar to the status update feature on the popular social networking site Facebook. Others use it to publish posts that offer useful information or commentary on particular topics.

Some do their Twitter posting with a desktop or laptop computer; others use their smartphones. Using these tools, people might publish to Twitter from home, an office, a coffee shop, a sidewalk, or even from a ferry, as one passenger did when he photographed US Airways Flight 1549 soon after it landed in the Hudson River in January 2009, posting a link to the photo on Twitter as the first photographic report from the scene.

Your audience, reporting live from the scene

When Whitney wrote in her first post that she was *live-Twittering*, she was referring to one of these many uses of the tool—to report live from a meeting, presentation, conference, or event (**Figure 1.2**).

FIGURE 1-2:
Whitney described
what she was doing.

With her short text dispatches she would describe what happened at the event like a journalist reporting live from the scene, but without the need for a satellite television truck.

Next, Whitney described her location: Pam's session that was titled *From Blog to Book Deal: How to* (**Figure 1.3**).

FIGURE 1-3:
Whitney described
where she was.

Many talented writers grow a substantial readership through the quality of their work on their blogs, and some of them have been able to extend their online readership into offline readership by getting a book deal with a mainstream publisher. Pam had personal experience in accomplishing the feat—she started her own blog, *Escape from Cubicle Nation*, to help people quit their corporate jobs and start their own ventures; and she recently managed to get a book of the same name published by Portfolio in 2009. Today's session was intended to help other aspiring writers learn how they might accomplish something similar.

But why would Whitney live-tweet in the first place, and who would find it useful?

An audience with an audience

It's not always easy to see the value of a Twitter post in isolation; rather, the value of a tweet lay in the eye of the beholder, and the meaning the tweet has to its author and reader. One of the ways people find value in using Twitter is when they *follow*, or subscribe to someone else's posts. This is a crucial concept that makes the difference between new users finding value in Twitter or abandoning it altogether.

When you first set up a Twitter account, you're not connected to anyone—you're like someone just arriving in a new city and you don't know a single person. But when you click the *Follow* button on someone else's Twitter home page, you establish a connection to them and agree to subscribe to the posts they publish. You might begin by following your friends' Twitter posts, and then you may expand your circle to follow people in your profession whom you respect, and then maybe you'll follow a celebrity or two.

As you grow the list of people you follow, you are creating a network that delivers to you only the posts you want to read from the people you trust. And just as you can follow other people, they can also follow you to receive information that you yourself publish.

For her readers who found the *Blog to Book* topic interesting, Whitney was providing a valuable service by passing on information about the event to those who could not be there in person. When she published her post, it was instantly viewable by her readers, and by anyone else searching the Twitter service. Twitter posts are usually public and viewable unless you take steps to make them private.

An audience looking you up online

The next part of Whitney's first Twitter post introduced to her readers today's presenters, who were all participants in a panel discussion (**Figure 1.4**).

FIGURE 1-4:
Whitney listed the members of the panel discussion.

When you sign up for a Twitter account, you choose a username or handle for your account. In some ways it is similar to an email address, except your Twitter address is your username preceded by an @ sign, and can only be used within the Twitter service. Some people use their full names as their Twitter usernames, like *@whitneyhess* herself. Others, like Hugh MacLeod, cartoonist and author of *Ignore Everybody* (Portfolio, 2009), use an alternate name—in his case, *@gapingvoid*.

Guy Kawasaki, founding partner of Garage Technology Ventures and author most recently of *Reality Check* (Portfolio, 2008), is *@guykawasaki*; and Stephanie Klein, the author of the blog *Greek Tragedy* as well as *Moose: A Memoir of Fat Camp* (William Morrow, 2008), is *@stephanieklein*. Kate Lee, a literary agent from ICM, is *@katelaurielee*; and Pam, who had invited the panelists to appear today, is *@pamslim*.

Listing all of the panelists' Twitter handles enabled anyone reading the post to quickly visit the panelists' Twitter home pages, read their biographies, or scan their recent posts and conduct other research on them.

Whitney extended her coverage of the event to the visual when she reached into her bag and took a picture of the panel and posted it on the popular photo-sharing website Flickr (**Figure 1-5**).

FIGURE 1-5:
In addition to live-Twittering the panel, Whitney took a photo of participants Hugh MacLeod, Guy Kawasaki, and Stephanie Klein and posted it on Flickr.
(Photo courtesy of Whitney Hess)

An audience creating a flow of information you're not creating or managing

If people find Twitter posts they like, it's fast and easy to follow their authors on the Twitter service; and it's just as easy to *un-follow* someone if the posts are not useful. As with traditional journalists, over time writers like Whitney develop a reputation for the topics and events they choose to report and the quality of their writing. Popular writers tend to act as trusted editors, selecting relevant information, insight, commentary, and additional resources that readers find interesting and useful. As Whitney cultivates her trusted reputation it helps her grow her base of followers—currently at 4,500—who remain followers because they want to hear more from her.

Sometimes Twitter writers include a link to a website—as in this example (**Figure 1.6**).

I'm live-Twittering "From Blog to Book Deal" with @gapingvoid @guykawasaki @stephanieklein @katelaurielee @pamslim http://is.gd/nM4E #sxswi

FIGURE 1-6:
Whitney provided a link to more resources.

Whitney wanted to share with her readers the direct web address of a page on the SXSW website that contained more detailed information about the panel. But a common problem that writers on Twitter run into is the excessive length of website addresses, such as the original one Whitney intended to share:

http://sxsw.com/interactive/talks/schedule?action=show&id=IAP0900156

With only 140 characters available for any post, the original URL would have used up 68 characters—almost half of her available space. So here Whitney used a *URL shortener* service called *is.gd*, which compressed the address to only 17 characters—*http://is.gd/nM4E*—a savings of 51 characters that she could use to include other useful information. Many third-party services that publish Twitter posts have URL shorteners built in, so you don't have to go to another website to accomplish the task.

Your audience is making their reporting easy to find

And finally, the last bit of text at the end of Whitney's post may look extraneous, but it packs a great deal of Twitter power (**Figure 1.7**).

The letters *#sxswi* are a *hashtag*—a special code that Twitter writers place in their posts to indicate they are attending or referring to a specific event or topic. In this case, people Twittering from the SXSW Interactive Festival would include *#sxswi* in their posts. When someone searches for that hashtag on Twitter, the results include the tweets with that term. In addition to event-wide hashtags like *#sxswi*, presenters like Pam sometimes provide audiences with a meeting-specific hashtag like *#blogtobook*, making posts for that meeting even easier to find on Twitter.

Whitney managed to pack quite a bit of meaning in the 138 characters of her Twitter post; and this was only the first of dozens more posts Whitney would write in the next hour as she live-Twittered the panel's presentation, all of which would reach her 4,500 followers.

Although Whitney was quite experienced at live-tweeting, she could not have predicted that the way she used Twitter that day would play a role in putting her on a dramatic collision course with one of the speakers on the panel.

The Seeds of Conflict

Having published her first Twitter post, Whitney looked up from her computer and was surprised there weren't more people in the room, so she posted her impressions (**Figure 1-8**).

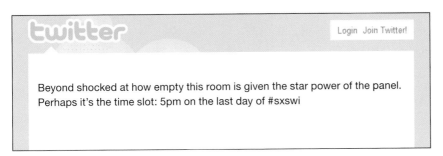

Beyond shocked at how empty this room is given the star power of the panel. Perhaps it's the time slot: 5pm on the last day of #sxswi

FIGURE 1-8:
Whitney expressed her surprise that there weren't more people there to see the well-known participants of the panel discussion.

The *Blog to Book* panel was slotted for the last hour of the last day of SXSW Interactive Festival. Eventually about 100 people would find their way to Room 18 by the time the session started.

Pam started off the panel by introducing herself and her fellow panelists, along with some of the members of the audience whom she knew. Pam asked the group how many people were bloggers, and most of the people in the room raised their hands. She then asked how many had written a book from their blog, and only a few raised their hands. From her poll, she knew she had a good match between the information she had planned for the session, and the audience who was there.

As moderator, Pam viewed her own role as the advocate for the audience, holding herself responsible for making sure their needs were being met by her and the panelists. Trained as a facilitator before she became a writer, Pam had a friendly, evenhanded demeanor as she guided the panel through a spirited discussion about how to write a book proposal, get the attention of a literary agent, and develop a strategy for getting published. Sometimes she asked a question to prompt a conversation, interjected a point, or guided the discussion to a new topic if the current one had run its course.

Mining for nuggets

Whitney had been especially interested in attending the *Blog to Book* panel because she had been following panelist Stephanie Klein's work for years, and now Whitney was keen to hear her in person tell her story about getting published.

When Stephanie described her excitement at hearing interest in her work from a publisher, Whitney quoted her in a Twitter post and used Stephanie's Twitter username for attribution (**Figure 1-9**).

As the discussion continued forward, the panelists shared their stories, advice, and sometimes conflicting strategies. Whitney mined the conversation for nuggets of advice about why bloggers should consider publishing books. For example, panelist Guy Kawasaki described the permanency of books compared to blogs, and Whitney reported it on Twitter (**Figure 1-10**).

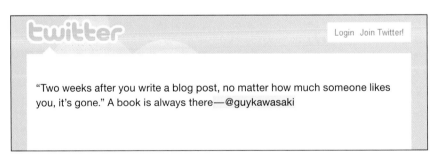

Whitney finds she gets much more from live-Twittering an event than she does from just sitting and listening—the act of processing, condensing, and publishing her tweets within a 140-character limit takes her through a process of engaging with the information at a deeper level than she otherwise would.

Next on the panel, Hugh described how his blog had facilitated a relationship with one of his readers, the popular marketing author Seth Godin, which was instrumental in getting Hugh's book published, as Whitney reported (**Figure 1-11**).

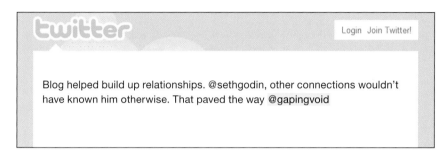

FIGURE 1-11:
Whitney para-
phrased advice
from panelist
Hugh MacLeod.

Throughout the session Whitney was looking for the practical marketing tips she could use herself and pass on to her readers. Stephanie, for example, worked hard to find innovative ways to market her blog, placing her blog web address everywhere she could, as Whitney reported (**Figure 1-12**).

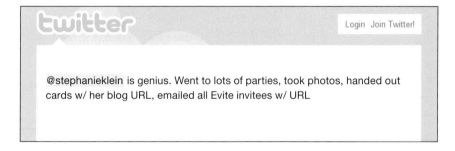

FIGURE 1-12:
Whitney praised
Stephanie Klein's
marketing tactics.

Over the course of the hour-long panel, Whitney would collect an impressive body of information via the 48 tweets she posted. Later, Whitney would copy and paste all of the Twitter posts on her regular long-form blog so her 10,000 blog readers could quickly scan the information to learn what happened. She would also add extended commentary and additional context to the entire stream of posts that would not be possible to include in single posts in isolation.

But a few of those posts Whitney would later regret.

Two different approaches

About 25 minutes into the session, Pam guided the discussion to the topic of whether a writer would get better results by investing time in cultivating relationships to get introductions to a publisher, or by investing time in writing a book proposal first. Guy and Hugh were advocates of working trusted connections to get to an agent. Taking a different view as a literary agent, Kate said she encourages book proposals, and is open to reading any that a writer sends her, as Whitney reported (**Figure 1-13**).

FIGURE 1-13:
Whitney para-
phrased advice
from panelist
Kate Lee.

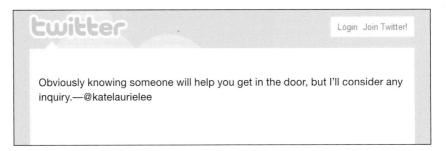

Obviously knowing someone will help you get in the door, but I'll consider any inquiry.—@katelaurielee

Kate described two routes she had seen by which writers turn their blogs into books:

- One route is when bloggers have a "fantastic idea"—some concept that is easy to see how it will turn into a book.
- The other route is when a blog reveals a "great voice"—the blogger is indeed a talented writer, but it is harder to identify exactly what the book will be.

Stephanie affirmed that the latter route applied in her case, and it had been extremely hard for her to prepare her own proposal, as Whitney reported (**Figure 1-14**).

FIGURE 1-14:
Whitney quoted
Stephanie about her
work on her book
proposal.

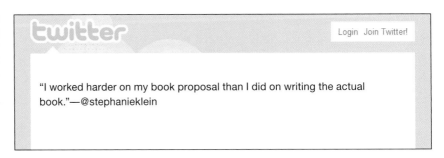

"I worked harder on my book proposal than I did on writing the actual book."—@stephanieklein

Kate said that she thought Guy and Hugh's experience of getting published through connections was uncommon, and that for someone like Stephanie the route was harder because she didn't already have an obvious book idea coming from her blog.

Guy disagreed with Kate, and Whitney expressed what she thought about the difference of opinion (**Figure 1-15**).

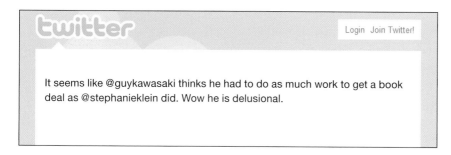

FIGURE 1-15:
Whitney tweeted
that she disagreed
with Guy.

Guy went on to explain his position in more detail as he talked on the panel.

> ...just like in the venture capital business there's one theory that you craft this great cover letter, this great business plan, this great pitch, you send it in and Trixie or Biff who is sitting at the front desk of Kleiner Perkins is going to open the envelope and be freaking blown away that you're going to be selling dog food online, that they're going to rush it in and show it to Michael Moritz or John Doerr. The other theory is…Seth knows him, and Seth calls up his editor and says, 'Listen, you know, Adrian, you gotta publish this book.' I would recommend that path. It's much higher probability.

Guy looked over at Hugh and said, "You probably didn't write a book proposal, did you?"

Hugh answered, "Nope."

Then Kate started making a point, "Yeah, but who, how many people have that…"

But Guy continued, "Let me finish. Let me finish. I know how you have to tell your story—how you're open, and you want to hear all these great things, I understand…"

Kate said, "No, the average person…"

But Guy went on, "I understand, I understand, because every venture capitalist says, 'Yeah, send me your plan; I always read my plans.' Bullshit. So the way it works, you can come away from this session thinking, it's who you know… More accurately it's not that…It's who knows about *you*."

Pam knew that Guy has strong opinions and a forceful personality, but from her judgment as moderator, carefully listening to his tone and watching the body language of the panelists, she didn't feel like Guy was being rude toward Kate or overstepping bounds to the point where Pam would need to say something.

Two different perceptions

Sitting in the front row as an audience member, Whitney perceived the situation completely differently. She felt that Guy was being chummy with the other male panelist, and now he was aggressively talking over a female panelist who was not challenging him on it. Obviously feeling strongly about the situation, Whitney posted on Twitter her take on what had happened (**Figure 1-16**).

FIGURE 1-16:
Whitney posted that she thought Guy was talking over other panel members.

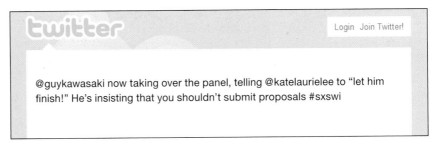

@guykawasaki now taking over the panel, telling @katelaurielee to "let him finish!" He's insisting that you shouldn't submit proposals #sxswi

Because Twitter allows you to post easily and instantly, posts sometimes can be emotional. What someone writes in the heat of the moment in a short Twitter post may not be the same thing she would write if she had time to think about things in a longer, more considered piece of writing. And at the moment, Whitney was unhappy with Guy and had a tool at hand to express how she felt.

When Guy is on stage giving a keynote he doesn't monitor what is being posted on Twitter because he considers it rude to do so. But because he was a panelist today he had the time to scan posts while other panelists were talking.

Still with her emotions rising, Whitney wrote a new post expressing her feelings about how she thought Guy was acting and clicked to publish it. She used a word she rarely says verbally, let alone in print.

Guy looked down at his computer and read the post from someone on Twitter he didn't know named @whitneyhess (**Figure 1-17**).

FIGURE 1-17:
Angry about what was happening, Whitney posted what she thought about Guy's behavior.

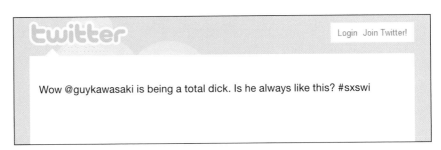

Wow @guykawasaki is being a total dick. Is he always like this? #sxswi

In an ordinary presentation, a presenter would only know if someone called him a crude name if she interrupted the session to say it. But because Guy was monitoring Twitter to see how the audience was reacting to the panel, he saw Whitney's comment.

> ## What Would You Do?
>
> If you were speaking to a group, and during the talk you saw a Twitter post from someone in the room that was critical of you, what would you do? Most Twitter posts are publicly published to the world, and they are archived and searchable at search.twitter.com. Would you ignore the post? Or would you say something? You'll find more scenarios like this one in Chapter 8 that you can rehearse in order to prepare for a range of backchannel comments.

When he read the post, Guy knew that anyone in the room—and the world, for that matter—could see it too because it had been published on Twitter. He strongly disagreed with Whitney's comment and felt like he was being wrongly portrayed.

In this critical moment on the stage, Guy faced a choice. He could ignore the post, which is often the best approach when facing a potentially volatile emotional situation. Or he could say something.

A number of forces had aligned in Room 18 that would make Guy decide what to do. It was the last panel of the last day of the event, Pam was a personal friend, he was feeling punchy, and he felt he didn't have anything to lose.

The audience talks back

Although he would never recommend anybody else do this, Guy looked out into the crowd in the room and in a loud voice he said, "I want to know who Whitney Hess is, because she just said I'm being a total dick. What is this?"

Surprised by Guy's statement, some people in the audience laughed.

A voice rang out from front row, center aisle, "I'm right here!"

As Guy started to speak, Whitney quickly added, "If I would've had a (microphone), I would've yelled it out!"

Pam's heart jumped in her throat for a second.

And everyone else sat on the edges of their seats waiting to hear what would happen next.

Introducing the Backchannel

The dramatic interaction unfolding in Room 18 of the Austin Convention Center is not the norm at most meetings and conferences today. Generally, people who present their ideas to a group can count on audience members to sit quietly in their chairs until they are dismissed or given permission to ask questions after viewing the Power-Point slides. But newly equipped with Twitter and tools like it, audiences are turning accepted social conventions upside down in an instant.

Although the audience's chairs in the room faced forward toward the primary conversation on the raised stage in the front of the room, there was a second, silent conversation happening in parallel at the back of the room. That's because Whitney wasn't the only person in the room creating a stream of information on Twitter—dozens of others in the room were doing the same thing.

Like Whitney, some of them were taking notes on the presentation and adding additional links, resources, and commentary for their followers to read. Some monitored all of the Twitter posts that had the session hashtag so they could read what their fellow audience members—including Whitney—were saying about the session. For example, Dave Gray posted on Twitter his surprise at Guy's comment (**Figure 1-18**).

FIGURE 1-18:
Dave Gray posted his surprise at the exchange between Guy and Whitney.

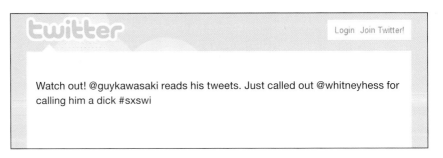

Login Join Twitter!

Watch out! @guykawasaki reads his tweets. Just called out @whitneyhess for calling him a dick #sxswi

Other audience members were *re-tweeting* posts—a term for re-posting someone's tweet and giving the original author credit. And some audience members were communicating with others in the room about the topic the panelists were discussing, as well as about unrelated topics.

A parallel conversation, inside the room and out

While these multiple streams of information flowed among the audience members and outward to the rest of the world outside the room, the speakers on the stage at the front of the room carried on their discussion about book publishing as they would in any other context.

But whether or not all of the panelists were aware, their audience actually was significantly larger than the 100 people there in Room 18. Via Whitney's Twitter stream, their ideas were reaching an additional 4,500 people following her posts. And in turn, every person using Twitter in the room was reaching their own followers. If one-quarter of the people in the room used Twitter and each had 300 followers who read all of their tweets, they would be reaching 7,500 people outside the room. Added to Whitney's audience, the total audience outside the room would be 12,000, or 120 times the size of the audience physically there.

When audience members create a line of communication like this to connect with others inside or outside of the room while a speaker is talking, they create a *backchannel*.

> **definition** ❯ A backchannel is a line of communication created by people in an audience to connect with others inside or outside the room, with or without the knowledge of the speaker at the front of the room. Usually facilitated by Internet technologies, it is spontaneous, self-directed, and limited in time to the duration of a live event. A backchannel can be constructive when it enhances and extends helpful information and relationships, and it can be destructive when it articulates and amplifies counterproductive emotions and sentiments.

The concept of a backchannel is not new—technically, passing a note written on a piece of paper to another audience member is a backchannel. In linguistics, backchannel refers to the verbal and nonverbal cues that a listener gives a speaker to indicate understanding or confusion. In diplomatic circles, a backchannel is a line of communication outside official channels; and in computer lingo, a backchannel may be the route by which a virus takes control of a compromised computer.

It was audiences at events in the technology industry mostly in the past decade who laid the framework for the backchannel. With the rise of the Internet, tech-savvy audience members found they could use a range of tools to create impromptu lines of communication, including Internet Relay Chat (IRC), live blogging, text messages, instant messages, email, and custom chat rooms. Instead of keeping their thoughts inside their heads or writing them in their personal notepads or computers, these audience members found they could use these new technologies to broadcast their thoughts to other people both inside the room and out, while the presentation was still happening.

But what was once the domain of the tech-savvy few is now becoming the domain of the many as more people discover they can easily use Twitter to create their own backchannel during live presentations. Twitter does have its limits, as we'll explore later, but its popularity is ushering in a new era of backchannel possibilities.

A double-edged sword

The early adopters discovered things that still hold true about the backchannel; specifically, that it can be constructive when it

- Enhances the information coming from the speaker, as people take notes, add commentary, and provide additional resources to what is being said at the front of the room.
- Connects people within a room, building communities around ideas.
- Connects people with others outside the room, as those not attending use technology to follow the dispatches from the live events, engage in conversations, and even directly ask questions of the presenters.
- Gives a speaker a new way to reach a wider audience.
- Provides a valuable archive of information to review after the event.

But they also found that a backchannel can be a double-edged sword, because it can be destructive when it

- Creates distraction as audience members pay attention to the backchannel more than the front of the room, or when the conversation strays to topics unrelated to the presentation at the hand.
- Leaves out of the conversation presenters or other audience members who are unaware or unable to join, creating a sense of unfairness because they have no way to respond to comments and criticisms.
- Lacks the ability to convey the full context for what is happening in a room because of the brevity of posts.
- Allows a rude or snarky tone to take hold of the conversation when people say things online that they would not say directly to a presenter.

Often a backchannel created by an audience happens in silence and is completely separate from the front channel coming from the stage. But when the backchannel and front channel collide, they can spill out into the open suddenly and unexpectedly, as they did at the *Blog to Book* panel.

The back of the room collides with the front

Whitney had been finding the backchannel a helpful tool that day to reach out to her readers, but she was now surprised that her post on Twitter had suddenly entered the room. After all, it's one thing to make a comment in the heat of the moment and post it on the Internet, but it's another thing to have that comment read by the speaker in front of the room of 100 people.

And now the words that were intended only for the virtual world suddenly came crashing into the flesh-and-blood world of Room 18.

Back from the Brink

The exchange between Guy and Whitney had knocked Pam momentarily off of her game—after all, most moderators aren't faced with the challenge of handling potentially explosive situations when there is a conflict between presenters and audiences on a public stage. Because of the extraordinary dynamics of the exchange, Pam's facilitation skills kicked into high gear as she became hyperaware of the tone of voice both Guy and Whitney were using, and carefully watched their body language for any clues on how they were feeling.

Pam was at the ready to cut off the interchange at any point if she felt it was getting out of hand or would potentially disrupt the panel.

After Guy and Whitney exchanged their initial words, Pam jumped in and asked, "What's going on?"

Guy said, "What...what is my dickiness?"

Whitney went on, "...that she was trying to say something and you were cutting her off."

Guy countered, "She was interrupting *me*! How many believe she was interrupting me?"

The audience laughed. Pam could see by Whitney's body language that she was surprised to be put on the spot and was uncomfortable in the situation.

Pam was conscious that she didn't want the audience to turn against Whitney and was not going to let that happen.

Whitney said, "I believe what was happening is… that we're trying to discuss how all of us as unknowns with blogs can find a way to get to a place where our blogs can become credible enough to turn into book proposals…."

Guy said, "Yeah…"

Whitney continued, "I understand that you have notoriety from prior work that you've done, right, so let's just get back to that, (instead of) 'Well, I know people'…"

Guy countered, "No. But wait. Hold on here. You've got me completely wrong. My colleague here from ICM was saying no matter who you are, send in a proposal, she reads it, blah blah blah…I'm telling you another way, if you're unknown, is to write good stuff and get known…"

Whitney responded, "That's actually not what you said. You told her, 'Yeah, yeah, yeah…VC's say that too, but that's not what they do…'"

Guy said, "We're in a parallel universe here!"

The audience laughed. Guy continued, "So what I'm suggesting is you write good stuff, you get known, and then people who are known will be happy to introduce you. That's what I'm suggesting."

Kate added, "Unless they're insecure…"

Guy said, "I can't help that. So that's a recommended path. You can go with her path. That path works. This is another path. Write good stuff and people like us who are published will know and we'll be glad to help you, for the reason that I would like to score karmic points and to have some favor that I can call back on my editor or agent some day. So in fact I'm giving you another path, which is quite the contrary to what you're saying I'm doing. So I don't believe I'm being a *dick*."

Guy pronounced the last word in a drawn-out, funny tone, prompting more laughter.

Then Pam decided it was time to cut off the exchange and continue on with the rest of the panel, so she said, "But I appreciate making sure that we keep that focus. I appreciate that, I really do. I love Twitter for that reason."

A crisis averted

Without missing a beat, Pam continued guiding the panel discussion on its course for another 20 minutes.

Meanwhile, Whitney continued posting on Twitter, including her thoughts about what had just happened (**Figure 1-19**).

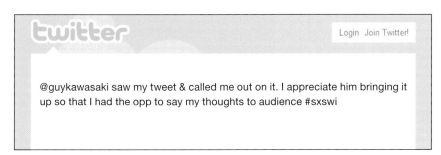

@guykawasaki saw my tweet & called me out on it. I appreciate him bringing it up so that I had the opp to say my thoughts to audience #sxswi

FIGURE 1-19: Whitney posted that there were no hard feelings after her exchange with Guy.

Pam's moderating skills, Guy's public speaking experience and positive tone, and Whitney's ability to have a frank discussion about something and move on were all contributors to keeping the panel on track.

The interaction may just come down to two people interpreting the same experience in two completely different ways. After the session, Whitney posted her thoughts on Twitter (**Figure 1-20**).

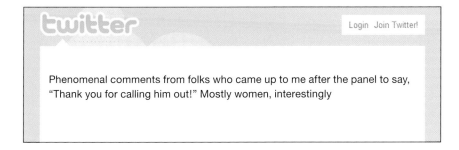

Phenomenal comments from folks who came up to me after the panel to say, "Thank you for calling him out!" Mostly women, interestingly

FIGURE 1-20: Whitney tweeted that she received positive comments from audience members.

And Guy said later in an email:

I chose to take on something that I thought was inaccurate. I did not interrupt the other speaker—she interrupted me. If someone wants to call me a dick, it should be true—at least at that instance in time.

Ultimately there were no hard feelings between Guy and Whitney, and Pam handled the situation effectively. No one raised their voice, and no one threw tomatoes.

But still, for the standards of presentations in the U.S. and many countries, the exchange was surprising and was a moment the audience would not soon forget.

Lesson(s) learned

Reflecting on the 2½-minute exchange, Pam thought it had not detracted from the session, but instead it had added an emotional lift to the panel at the point where energy was starting to drag.

And it offered a chance for everyone to learn something about how to engage the backchannel.

Lessons from *Blog to Book*

When Pam arrived in the room, she used her laptop to display her PowerPoint slides, so she was not able to use the computer to get online and monitor the backchannel on Twitter. Her lesson learned—a moderator should have a laptop or other device available to monitor what people are saying in the backchannel during

a presentation. Whitney never expected Guy to read her comment, let alone read it to the audience. She is now very conscious of what she posts when she live-Twitters from an event, only writing comments in a way that she would be comfortable having the presenter read to the group.

Whitney's final post on Twitter wrapped up her impressions of what had happened that day (**Figure 1-21**).

FIGURE 1-21: Whitney tweeted that the panel was useful.

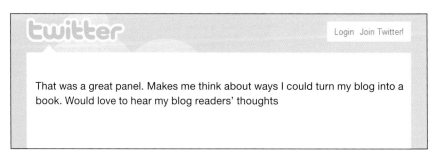

> That was a great panel. Makes me think about ways I could turn my blog into a book. Would love to hear my blog readers' thoughts

But that wouldn't be the last thought on the topic.

Although the backchannel primarily takes place during a live presentation, it will often prompt a conversation that continues after the session has ended. A few days after the *Blog to Book* panel, blogger Eileen Corrigan wrote an extended post about her impressions of the session and sent a link to it to her followers on Twitter (**Figure 1-22**).

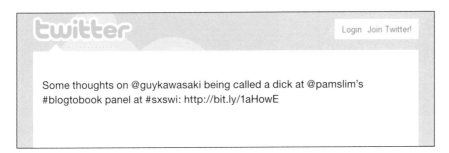

Guy commented on Eileen's blog post, as did Pam, and the lively conversation continued there over a few days; prompting several readers to note that the quality of the discussion there was impressive.

Another attendee, Austin Kleon, had taken sketch notes during the *Blog to Book* session, then afterward scanned the graphic in his sketchbook and used Twitter to send his followers a link to the image on Flickr (**Figure 1-23**).

This is just one more example of the creative and interesting ways the backchannel uses a range of technology and tools to report on live presentations, in addition to Twitter, photographs, audio and video podcasts, and live-streaming video.

A New View from the Podium

The history of the technology-aided backchannel is brief, but the rapidly growing phenomenon indicates that something fundamental is changing—the relationship among event organizers, presenters, and audiences. Just as the interaction in Room 18 demonstrated, differing points of view can bring presentations to the brink of dramatic and public breakdowns of communication.

But the potential for positive outcomes is equally attention-worthy, as we all find our way across the front lines of this rapidly shifting landscape known as the backchannel. There have been occasional disruptive technologies that have transformed the field of presentations—the introduction of blackboards, microphones, overhead projectors, video, and PowerPoint presentation software. Only the next few years will tell whether audiences use Twitter to make simple adjustments to the way we do presentations, or radically reshape them altogether.

One thing is sure already: the backchannel is rewriting the job description of everyone involved with presentations, including hosts, audiences, and presenters. Hosts have to rethink the way they create to bring presenters and audiences together. Audiences have to carefully consider the new power in their hands, and how to use it wisely and effectively. But it is presenters whose jobs will change the most, because they are looking at a rapidly changing world from the view of the podium.

Presenters, meet your new audiences

How much change are you looking at if you're a presenter today? If your audience members have created a backchannel, it's likely they are

- Typing into laptops and texting on smartphones instead of sitting quietly looking at you or taking notes on paper.
- Recording everything you say in writing, photographs, audio, and video.
- Talking about you to other people inside and outside the room before, during, and after your presentation—possibly praising or criticizing you.
- Asking questions during a talk instead of waiting until the end.

- Checking your facts in real time, and calling you out if they question your credibility.
- Gauging your demeanor and attitude, and challenging you if they feel you lecture, pontificate, use corporate speak, or are otherwise inauthentic, condescending, patronizing, rambling, or verbose.
- Sometimes walking out of your presentation if they don't think it's a good fit for them; and sometimes walking into the room during your presentation if they've heard good things about it in the backchannel.
- Perhaps getting mad about something you said, and thinking about interrupting your presentation or confronting you, and on rare occasions even trying to take control and derail your presentation.

The backchannel is the future

You may not yet have had a backchannel in your presentation, but you will soon enough. And when it arrives, it will be here to stay.

Communications expert Jen McClure says she would have been surprised two years ago if someone said speakers would be looking at screens instead of at her, but now she expects it. "As speakers, there are just different expectations," Jen said. "There's no going back to where we were at." Jen explained that audiences simply aren't going to close their laptops and that "anyone who rejects it outright may lose audiences."

Author Dan Gillmor agrees that although speakers may not like it, the backchannel is here to stay. "Welcome to real life," said Dan. "Anyone who is teaching is painfully aware that students are IM'ing like crazy and talking about things relevant or not, behind the back of the speaker. This is common. The fact (is) that people can do it, so live with it. Be compelling as a speaker and I'll pay attention to you."

Seeing an opportunity to join something bigger

The seminal book *The Cluetrain Manifesto* (Basic Books, 2000) described 10 years ago that as the Internet has given people the ability to express themselves, a global conversation has begun. In this highly connected age, people are already talking about you, so you might as well be part of the conversation.

Entrepreneur Loïc Le Meur says, "If no one Twitters about it, it's a disaster. Even if it's negative, it's good, because it means it matters."

Of course conversations have always been around, it's just that now they take place everywhere on the planet there is a computer with an Internet connection.

When you look at the backchannel as part of a conversation that's already been happening, but now it's in a new form, it's not as daunting. You can simply use new tools and actually create a bigger conversation than ever before possible. Besides, if you don't engage the backchannel, you potentially have something to lose. You won't know what's happening in the room or what your audience is thinking and saying. You may lose opportunities offered by people who search speakers' reputations on Twitter before they hire speakers, or who expect them to be savvy about how to use technologies to engage their audiences. And you stand to lose your credibility or hard-earned reputation if people you have yet to meet search Twitter and define who you are based on negative backchannel comments they find.

A genie not going back in the bottle

You may think you can wait a while to engage the backchannel, because you haven't yet seen any of your audiences set one up during a presentation. But the situation could change at the click of the mouse. Whitney, Guy, and Pam were at an event where a wireless Internet connection, laptops, mobile phones, and Twitter are the norm. But that technology toolkit is rapidly becoming standard for audience members everywhere, whatever profession they are in and wherever they may be. Ready or not, you may have a backchannel waiting for you at your next presentation.

You may be concerned about whether engaging the backchannel is something you can even do. After all, you may already be overwhelmed by the fear of public speaking and the daunting task of creating a presentation with a good story, solid material, and quality graphics. And now, on top of that tall order, you have to quickly learn new tools, new skills, and new approaches to presentations, likely adding stress to an already difficult experience.

It's true that the backchannel can make your job harder. But it can also make your job much easier. If you engage the changes and learn how to use the new tools at your fingertips, you can pave the way to a new, more conversational form of communicating. Not only will you gain a live, searchable database of your audience's thoughts, but you also get immediate feedback and build a platform that will extend your ideas far outside the room, with far greater impact.

Presenting some fundamental questions

As we all move forward into the new era of the backchannel, we're entering new and uncharted waters. As the *Blog to Book* panel demonstrated, the backchannel is sometimes a surprising and even shocking place, and in the wake of the change it is creating, it is raising fundamental questions that we don't have the answers to yet, including

- What do audiences expect today?
- What are the ground rules?
- Who is accountable?
- What is the best structure for a presentation?
- What is the best way to integrate an audience's feedback?
- How do you prevent distraction, rudeness, and loss of control?
- When is a backchannel appropriate, and when is it not?

In this book, we'll address all of these questions and explore possible answers together.

But be assured, as you engage the tectonic shifts afoot, you'll be able to surf the coming backchannel wave safely to shore and get back up and jump right in again.

2

How to Join a Twitter Backchannel

Only a few simple steps
are needed to begin participating
in a Twitter backchannel

oom 18 of the Austin Convention Center was just one place where an audience used technology to create a backchannel—it's happening all over the world.

The popular U.S. television show *American Idol* asks audience members to cast votes for contestants using text messaging. In Japan, concert organizers invite audience members to use text messaging to vote to keep popular bands on the stage longer, or to vote unpopular bands off the stage sooner. In Scandinavia, audiences have been using text messaging for years to express their opinions in just about every possible social context. And in business conference rooms, people from the same company will use BlackBerry devices to communicate vital information with one another in the middle of negotiations with another company.

Although people have created backchannels for years and continue to do so with a range of tools, there is one tool in particular that is turning a once-obscure activity into a phenomenon—Twitter.

The Backchannel and the Rise of Twitter

According to comScore, more than 50 million people worldwide visited the Twitter website (**Figure 2-1**) in June 2009, and that number doesn't include the more than half of Twitter users who don't go to the website at all.

FIGURE 2-1:
The Twitter home page

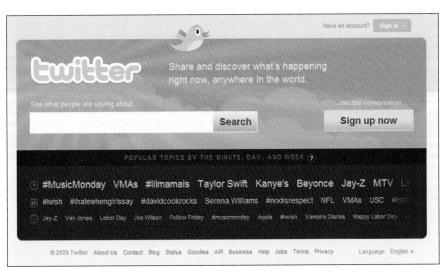

Twitter is clearly a phenomenon that is changing the way people communicate, as people use it in every conceivable situation.

Television news broadcasters give out their Twitter addresses so viewers will send comments. Church pastors encourage congregants to use Twitter to give them live feedback during services. Company CEO's send tweets to customers to ask for their opinions about products and services. Celebrities give fans day-by-day updates on their lives, bypassing the need to use mainstream media. Even members of Congress used Twitter to create a backchannel during U.S. President Barack Obama's address to Congress in January 2009. And some educators have been experimenting with using Twitter and other social media technologies to introduce a backchannel to the class-room, a practice that has generated intense criticism from those who see it as a threat to traditional lecture formats and established pedagogy.

Twitter may be fast becoming a household name, but using it to create a backchan-nel is still something new to most audience members. Who are these people who are creating Twitter backchannels?

Surveying the Twitter audience

One thing we know for sure about the backchannel is that we don't know much for sure. The use of the backchannel is so new that there is little research on the topic; the few studies that have been conducted have analyzed small numbers of backchannel comments to categorize the types of posts people write or how frequently they post.

Most early uses of the backchannel were confined to people using Internet Relay Chat at technology conferences or other chat tools in experimental classrooms, rather than in more mainstream settings. But now that more people are using Twitter as a backchannel, there are general things we do know about the group who uses that particular tool.

Data from comScore in April 2009 found that "it is the 25- to 54-year-old crowd that is actually driving this (Twitter) trend," with 45- to 54-year-olds 36 percent more likely than average to visit Twitter, followed by 25- to 34-year-olds, who are 30 percent more likely. This is contrary to conventional wisdom that younger people are driving social media trends, which may be due in part to the degree to which Twitter has been embraced by businesses.

A February 2009 study released by the Pew Internet & American Life Project found that people who use Twitter and similar social media tools are a more mobile group, likely to use laptops, handhelds, and cell phones to communicate, and though they use technology at the same rates as other Internet users…

...the ways in which they use the technology—to communicate, gather, and share information—reveals their affinity for mobile, untethered, and social opportunities for interaction. Moreover, Twitter as an application allows for and enhances these opportunities, so it is not so surprising that users would engage in these kinds of activities and also be drawn to an online application that expands those opportunities.

Those opportunities include bringing laptops and smart phones into your next presentation.

Using Twitter in conferences

Though the backchannel is not limited to meeting rooms and conference centers, those have been the places where the backchannel has started to shake the foundations of public speaking to the core.

In early 2009 the public relations firm Weber Shandwick released the results of a survey of global conference organizers that indicated 58 percent more blogging and Twittering was happening during conferences than three years prior.

Of course people use Twitter in many different ways, not everyone who uses Twitter uses it to join a backchannel, and the service is only one of many people use to create a backchannel.

But it's safe to say that when your audience includes people 25 to 54 years old, and there is a wireless or mobile phone connection in the room, some people in the audience will likely be using Twitter or a similar service to create backchannel communication.

The spontaneous rise of Twitter backchannels

A backchannel can spring out of nowhere, originated by only a few audience members, or it can be the result of extensive forethought and planning. The basic ingredients that need to be in place are audience members who want to communicate with one another while a presenter is speaking, and their communication tools—usually a laptop or smartphone, wireless or mobile phone service, and Twitter.

In many instances, audiences decide to set up a backchannel informally, with little or no planning. Someone attending an event will just make up an event hashtag and start including it in Twitter posts.

Word spreads rapidly and virally—others who read the posts will see the hashtag and begin including it in their posts, and soon many at the event on Twitter will be using it. Once audience members have a hashtag to use on Twitter, there's no additional setup required, and the backchannel is open for business.

By its nature, an unofficial backchannel is usually

- Voluntary.
- Ad hoc.
- Spontaneous.
- Grassroots.
- Unmanaged.
- Temporary.

Where a meeting host usually makes decisions to formalize and plan the way the event will work, the unofficial backchannel forms outside of any established arrangements and is outside of the hosts' or presenters' control, authority, and ability to manage. Hosts and presenters often are completely unaware that there is a backchannel in the room. Sometimes it doesn't matter, but other times their lack of awareness can have disastrous consequences, as we'll explore later.

Hosts and presenters who have seen the positive value of backchannels at meetings will proactively help audience members to create and use these alternative communication systems. With the backchannel in mind, they may ensure there is wireless service available for people to use. They will create an event hashtag well in advance of the event and publicize it in marketing materials, so the audience does not have to make one up. And in some instances they may provide the technical setup for a backchannel outside of Twitter; for example, hosts concerned about privacy may set up a password-protected chat room available only to the audience and publicize the login information only to the audience in the room.

Choosing Twitter as a Backchannel Tool

Twitter was not created for people to use during live presentations, yet audiences nevertheless have rapidly adopted it the past two years as the tool of choice for creating their own backchannels.

Twitter is the backchannel tool *du jour* because it is

- Free.
- Easy to set up.
- Easy to use.
- Fast.
- Searchable.
- Able to display thumbnail photos of members.
- Open to anyone who wants to join in a conversation.
- Accessible on smart phones in addition to laptops.
- Capable of facilitating an ongoing relationship among audience members long after a meeting has ended.

But when it comes to setting up a backchannel, Twitter is not the only game in town.

Other backchannel tools

At its simplest level, two people could create a backchannel by passing a note on a piece of paper during a meeting. But the range of Internet tools vastly expands people's ability to communicate.

The most popular tool to create a backchannel before Twitter was a *chat room*, which allow you to create an online space where meeting participants can discuss a presentation. Internet Relay Chat has been a popular choice over the years, and more recent chat tools include Tinychat (**Figure 2-2**), Chatzy, Meebo, Chatango, TweetChat, ChatMaker, Today's Meet, SavorChat, BackNoise, and the host of chat tools that come with web services such as Google.

Some audiences use *document sharing* tools such as Google Docs and EtherPad to set up a single document that multiple people can access simultaneously. Others use instant messaging services or group text messaging services such as TXTMob. Some people use live-blogging—posting on their regular blog throughout an event. Others use simple email to create a backchannel.

> **tip ❭** The list of tools you can use to create a backchannel is constantly evolving as new companies enter the scene, others leave, and existing tools change. Visit www.backchannelbook.com for the latest list of tools, and if there's one not on the list, you're welcome to add it.

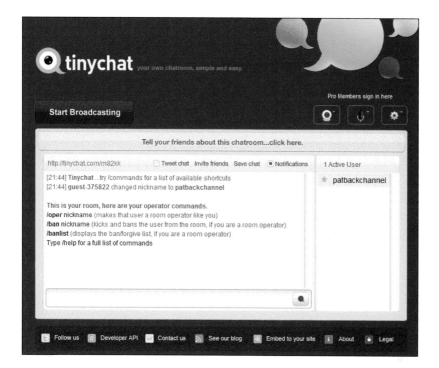

FIGURE 2-2:
Tinychat is one of
many tools besides
Twitter you can
use to create a
backchannel.

Shortcomings of Twitter as a backchannel tool

No tool is perfect for creating a backchannel. Even Twitter has its shortcomings. Audiences who use Twitter during live events report that it can be

- Difficult to carry on a conversation because posts are not threaded.
- Unmanageable when too many people post on a topic.
- Meaningless when the posts are not relevant to your interests.
- Confusing because of the use of abbreviations and jargon.
- Lacking the context of the original source material from the presentation.
- Redundant when followers receive multiple posts from people attending the same event.
- Off-putting when only a few people use it and share insider jokes.
- Frustrating to try to figure out the big picture of what is happening.

It's possible that Twitter will add new features that solve these problems, or another tool may replace it altogether.

But even if Twitter goes away tomorrow, the tool has put changes in motion that will continue to impact audiences and how they create and use the backchannel.

That's why it's important that no matter what tool you use, you at least prepare yourself to join a Twitter backchannel.

How Do You Know Which Backchannel Tool To Use?

When you choose a tool to use for creating a backchannel, consider some of the following criteria:

Popularity: What tools are most people using?

Cost: How much are you willing to spend?

Ease of use: How easy is it for people to set up?

Skills required: What level of technical knowledge is required to use it?

Privacy: Do you need it to be password-protected, or is public OK?

Learning curve: Do people need to learn something new, or do they have something already that does the job?

Context: Do you want the backchannel to be a stand-alone space, or part of the flow of information someone gets through a service like Twitter?

Archiving: Do you want the information to be archived, or just temporary?

Identity requirements: Can users be anonymous, or do they have to identify themselves with a photo or other means?

Mobile accessibility: Can people use it on smart phones in addition to laptops?

Length of posts: Can people write their thoughts in long form, or will their posts be restricted in length?

It's easy to see why so many people are flocking to Twitter to set up or join a backchannel—because doing so is as simple as 1-2-3.

Step 1: Open Up a Twitter Account

If you don't already have a Twitter account, open a browser and visit www.twitter.com. (If you already have an account, skip to the next section.)

1. Click the "Sign up now" button.

   The "Join the Conversation" page appears (**Figure 2-3**), where you'll create your account.

2. In the "Full name" field, enter your first and last name.

3. In the Username field, enter the unique name that you want to appear on all of your Twitter posts (preceded by the @ sign). This could be your real name

(such as *whitneyhess* or *guykawasaki*), or it could be an online identity you want to use (such as *pistachio* or *gapingvoid*).

4. After you choose a password, enter your email address and type the security validation words.

5. Click "Create my account."

tip ❯ Try to keep your username to as few characters as possible. When someone else mentions your username or sends you a message on Twitter, the characters in your username count against the total character limit (140) of a post.

FIGURE 2-3:
The Twitter account setup page

You'll receive a welcome email that confirms your account was created.

Congratulations! You are now part of the Twitter community. But before you use the tool to join a backchannel, be sure to review some of your account settings, as described next.

Establish your identity

Now take a few minutes to establish your identity on Twitter so other audience members or presenters will know who you are.

1. After you log in to Twitter with your username and password, click the Settings button at the upper right of the page, which will lead you to your main account page. Here you'll see your name, username, and email address.

   Next, add information that will help people know who you are and how they can find more information about you.

2. In the "More info URL" field, type the address of your professional or personal website.

3. In the One Line Bio, describe who you are in 160 characters or less, and then fill in your Location.

4. At the bottom of the page, leave the "Protect my updates" box unchecked to have your Twitter posts publicly viewable and searchable.

5. Click Save.

   You'll see the results in your bio box, as shown in the upper right of your public Profile page (**Figure 2-4**).

   When you post something interesting and someone wants to find out more about you, they'll click through to your bio.

> **Name** Pat Backchannel
> **Location** Los Angeles, CA
> **Web** http://www.backch...
> **Bio** Speaker, author and
> hiking enthusiast

FIGURE 2-4:
Your Twitter bio

6. Now that you're done updating information on the Account tab, click the Picture tab to add a photograph to your profile (**Figure 2-5**).

Every Twitter post you publish includes a thumbnail version of your photo, so pick something that will be clear when it's significantly reduced in size.

FIGURE 2-5:
Adding your picture

This thumbnail photo is one of the features that makes Twitter so popular as a backchannel—whatever you write, people will be able to quickly see a photo of the person who wrote it, making Twitter a more personal place than most other tools you could use.

Your account has other settings you can personalize later, but for now let's get you connected.

Write your first tweet

To write your first tweet:

1. Click in the text box at the top of your Home page (**Figure 2-6**).

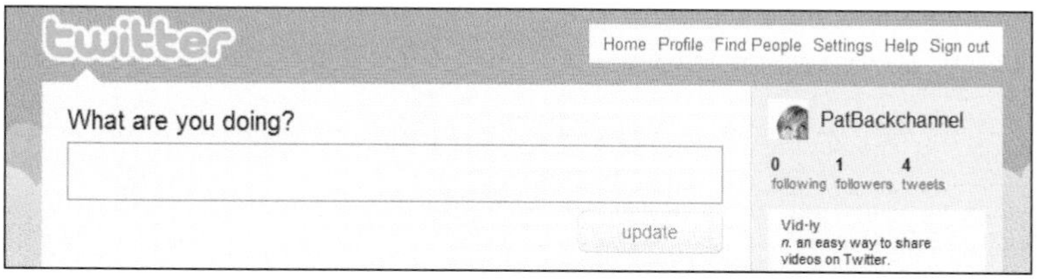

FIGURE 2-6:
The Twitter posting box

2. Write a tweet. Feel free to ignore the "What are you doing?" question in the posting box. Instead, answer "What can I say to be helpful?" or "How can I add value?"

3. A the end of your tweet, add an event hashtag. If you have an event coming up that has a hashtag, include that one; otherwise you can create your own by adding a series of letters after the # sign. The upcoming example includes the hashtag #XYZ.

4. Click the Update button to publish your tweet to the Twitter service.

   Now that you've sent your first backchannel tweet out into the world, take a look at how the world will see it.

5. Click the Profile button at the upper right of the page. Your tweet appears here on your Profile page in what is called your *timeline*—a chronological display of your tweets with the most recent at the top. As you write more tweets, you'll be able to read them from top to bottom (**Figure 2-7**).

Your own Home page on Twitter features the posts of people you follow, but when anyone else visits your Twitter page, they will see your Profile page and only the posts you wrote. Anyone visiting your Profile page can scroll through them to get a quick sense of who you are by what you write about, your style, and the usefulness of your tweets.

FIGURE 2-7: A Twitter timeline

Step 2: Preview a Backchannel Twitterstream

The real impact of your backchannel post becomes clearer when you visit the Twitter search page at http://search.twitter.com. Think of this page as Google search, except it searches only for Twitter posts.

To test it out, click inside the box, type the event hashtag you included in your tweet (**Figure 2-8)** (or type your own name or the event name), and then click the Search button.

FIGURE 2-8:
Searching for an
event hashtag

You'll quickly get a search results page. The one shown in **Figure 2-9** is an example of a search for *#NECC09*, the event hashtag for the National Educational Computing Conference held in Washington, D.C., in the summer of 2009.

This search results page is a display of this specific event's Twitter backchannel. Here you can see all posts that include the event hashtag up to the moment of your search, including the post you just published.

Unlike typical search engines that take some time to index web pages before they show up in search results, Twitter makes your posts available for searching almost immediately, available to anyone anywhere in the world with web access.

Depending on the hashtag you used, you may see only one or a few posts, or you may see hundreds.

FIGURE 2-9:
The real-time search results page for hashtag #NECC09 displays all tweets related to that hashtag.

As you scroll through the results, you're seeing the other members of your backchannel community for that event and getting to know them through the information each post includes

- A thumbnail photo of the author.
- The Twitter username of the author; if you click it, you'll go to the person's Home page, where you can see his or her bio and other posts.
- The text of the post, including the hashtag.

Below the text of each tweet you'll also see

- When it was posted.
- What tool was used to post the tweet.
- A Reply link; when you click it, you'll see a screen where you can write a message back to the author.
- A View Tweet link; when you click it, you'll see the post on a single page.

Although the search results page displays tweets up to the moment you clicked the Search button, people continue to post after you performed your search. You'll know that more search results have appeared when you see a yellow bar at the top of the page (**Figure 2-10**). Click the Refresh link to see an updated page that includes the latest posts.

FIGURE 2-10:
When new posts are
added to Twitter,
you'll receive a
notification; click
Refresh to see the
latest results.

> **Real-time results for #comiccon**   ⊕ Save this search
>
> 25 more results since you started searching. Refresh to see them.

During an event you can continue to refresh your page manually, install a browser add-in to do it for you, or use one of the many third-party tools that automatically refresh search results (visit www.backchannelbook.com for a list).

As you refresh your search results from the hashtag, you are displaying a *Twitterstream*—real-time, continuous flow of information from the event. Although it may only be a trickle, and you're just dipping your toes into it for now, during a live event a Twitterstream can be a rushing torrent of information that you will likely find useful. We'll explore this concept in the next chapter.

Monitoring multiple events, topics, and backchannels

The search you conducted for your event hashtag created a display of the Twitter backchannel for that single event, but there are instances where you'll want to monitor more than just one hashtag. For example, you may want to set up a search for an event hashtag to participate in the Twitter backchannel for your event, and also to monitor any mentions of you or your company.

If you visit http://search.twitter.com, you're only able to set up a single search, but other tools help make the job of setting up your searches easier. Free tools like Seesmic Desktop and TweetDeck (**Figure 2-11**) access the Twitter service and use multiple columns to display Twitter searches in a single window.

FIGURE 2-11:
TweetDeck allows you to set up multiple columns based on different search terms, including your event hashtag.

To use one of these tools, you'll first need to download it and set it up using your Twitter username and password. Then set up a search for your event hashtag to create a single persistent column that continuously searches for the term. Next, set up a search for a different term, such as your own name, to create a second column. Then create a search for another term, such as your organization's name, to create a third column. A horizontal scroll bar will allow you to scroll across columns if you create more than you can view in a single screen.

Accessing Twitter on Mobile Devices

Armed with a smart phone and a Twitter client such as TweetDeck for the iPhone (**Figure 2-12**), many audience members have the ability to participate in the backchannel without carrying a laptop or visiting the Twitter website.

Step 3: Begin Growing a Twitter Community

As described in Chapter 1, the real power of Twitter comes from the connections you have with others—both the people you follow and the people who follow you.

The concept of following

When you wrote your first tweet, it's likely no one else read it. That's because when you tweet something, people will read it if they follow you and happen to see your tweet as they scan the tweets of all the people they follow. Or, they might find it if they were searching Twitter for a particular topic included in your tweet.

But even with no followers, you are still able to join a backchannel, because all you need to do is search the hashtag for an event to display the live Twitterstream from the event.

What you do next in regards to growing a community depends on what you'd like to get from using Twitter.

Many people create a Twitter account and choose only to follow other people. According to an analysis by web security firm Purewire that was reported by TechCrunch in June 2009, 80 percent of Twitter accounts have fewer than 10 followers, and 30 percent have zero followers. Simply following others may work well for audience members who are happy to read what presenters, hosts, and others are tweeting, and to occasionally participate in a backchannel. For them, they would just focus on finding interesting people to follow and using event hashtags to join backchannels.

Other people choose to use Twitter as a broadcast medium, writing frequent tweets and aiming to collect a large number of followers. This is a smaller group; according to separate studies by Sysomos and Harvard Business School, approximately the top 10 percent of tweeters do 90 percent of the tweeting. Tweeting frequently and collecting followers is a good idea for hosts who want to market their events and attract attendees, or for presenters who want to spread their ideas and maintain an ongoing presence online.

Either way you'd like to go, a few Twitter features can help you get started with following others or inviting others to follow you.

Following other people

The Twitter service makes it easy for you to find people you'd like to follow.

1. To start making connections, at the top right of the page, click Find People to open a page like the one shown in **Figure 2-13**.

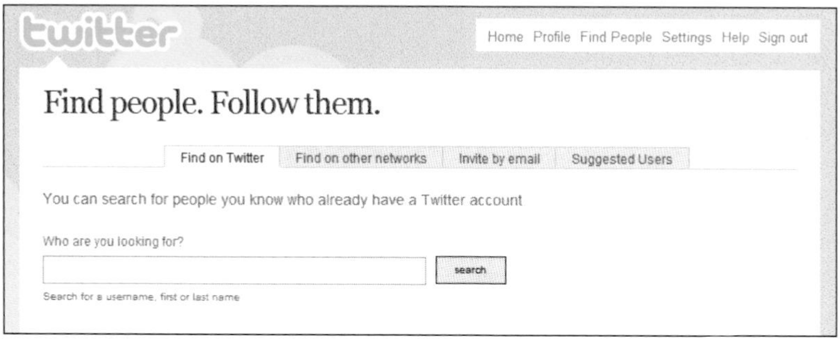

FIGURE 2-13:
The Find People page

2. Click the Suggested Users tab, and as you scroll through the list, select the individuals or organizations that you find interesting. Then click the Follow button.

3. Click Find People again, and on the "Find on Twitter" tab, type the name of a colleague you admire.

4. When you arrive on the Profile page, click the Following tally below his or her username.

5. Scroll through the list of people your colleague is following, and if any of them look interesting, click the Follow button to subscribe to their tweets.

Persuading other people to follow you

Though it's easy to follow other people, it's harder to get people to follow you because you have to persuade them to do so.

One way to get started is to use Twitter to invite people you already know. To invite people to follow you through various email services, choose the "Find on other networks" tab. Or to import email addresses of people you'd like to invite to follow you, click the "Invite by email" tab.

To persuade others to follow you and keep following, you'll need to tweet high-quality material on a regular basis. A quick web search about growing your list of Twitter followers will produce some excellent resources, but for hosts and speakers you'll want to focus on ways to attract followers who will attend your upcoming events.

> **tip ❯** For more detailed instructions about how to make the best use of Twitter and to grow a community, pick up a copy of *The Twitter Book* by Tim O'Reilly and Sarah Milstein (O'Reilly, 2009).

For example, if you're a host you may want to attract Twitter followers to your account as part of your event marketing plan. You'll want to make it as easy as possible for potential attendees to subscribe by including your Twitter username and hashtag in all of your communications such as email, print, and online advertisements. The type of tweets that will likely attract followers would be regular updates about the schedule, discount offers, and a series of tweets that introduces your speakers, topics, and value to potential attendees.

> **tip ❯** If you're a host, consider creating a Twitter account as the official source of all news about the event. Publicize the account and encourage participants to follow it—it's a powerful tool to publicize your event beforehand, to post up-to-the-minute news during the event, and to send out resources and follow-ups afterward. If you're a presenter or audience member, be sure to follow your host's Twitter account.

As a presenter you may also have a marketing plan in place to attract Twitter followers, and you'll also want to make it as easy as possible for people to follow you. One immediate thing you can do is include your Twitter username in all of your communications such as newsletters, websites, blogs, business cards, and email footers. Later, we'll look at ways you can use Twitter to reach out to potential audience members and attract more followers. For example, you should reach out to other Twitter users in your topic area and hold conversations with them to create awareness. Or if you're speaking at a specific event, you may consider a series of tweets in advance of the event to clarify the value of your talk, build anticipation, and link people to resources they can review in advance.

The Rewards and Risks
of the Backchannel

By following the steps in this chapter, you've done everything you need to do to join a Twitter backchannel. And with those few keystrokes, you are on the way to changing the world of presentations forever.

Next we'll look at the potential rewards of a backchannel in Chapter 3 and the potential risks in Chapter 4, before diving in to the hands-on things you can do to engage the backchannel in Chapter 5 onward.

3

The Rewards of the Backchannel

A backchannel changes the dynamics
of traditional presentations and offers
a range of potential rewards to both
presenters and audiences

W hen people hear stories about Twitter and the backchannel, it's easy to jump to conclusions about what it is, what it does, and whether it's a good or bad thing. But it's only when you actually see it in action that you can get a sense of its many possibilities.

A Cure for Hiccups, or a Presentation Revolution?

The New York Times columnist David Pogue described in his blog *Pogue's Post* what he did with Twitter during a keynote presentation:

> *At one point, I figured that the best way to explain Twitter was to demonstrate it, live, on the big screen at the front of the ballroom. So I flipped out of PowerPoint and typed this to my Twitter followers: "I need a cure for hiccups... RIGHT NOW! Help?" I hit Enter. I told the audience that we would start getting replies in 15 seconds, but it didn't even take that long. Here are some of the replies that began scrolling up the screen:*
>
> - *florian: Put a cold spoon on your back—that's what my grandfather would do for hiccups.*
> - *michaeljoel: drop a lit match in a glass of water to extinguish it. take out match. drink water.*
> - *jbelmont: Simple. Just hold your breath until Windows 7 is released.*
> - *warcand: check your 401K. That should scare the hiccups right out of ya!*
> - *JuanluR: eat a full spoon of crushed ice.*
>
> *Has there ever been a wittier, smarter bunch (or a better collection of hiccup cures)? The audience and I were marveling and laughing at the same time. This was it: harnessing the power of the Web, the collective wisdom of strangers, in real time! The Twitterers of the world did not let us down. (And yes, I realize that this demo might not be as effective if you have, say, 20 followers instead of hundreds.)*

In Chapter 1, using Twitter changed the relationship between presenter and audience, and here David used Twitter to change the relationship between his audience in the room and his followers who were outside of the room. These two groups don't normally interact during live presentations, but through David and his Twitter post, they suddenly intersected, to the delight of his audience.

Because David had become a trusted source of information to his Twitter followers, he could count on them when he needed a hand—whether a simple request like a cure for hiccups, or later perhaps something more complex like researching a topic or getting to know an audience.

You may not ever do a live demonstration like David did on a stage, but you still can run experiments to demonstrate the impact of a backchannel. For example, to experiment with the backchannel I attended a presentation in Los Angeles by a speaker who said he doesn't use Twitter, and quite frankly, didn't see the point. As he gave his presentation, I took notes on my laptop using Twitter, posting some useful comments he made. Someone in St. Louis re-tweeted a post he found useful; and another person in the San Francisco Bay area posted that he thought the posts were interesting.

When one of my Twitter followers in New Zealand questioned one of the points the presenter made that I had tweeted, I held up my hand in the room in Los Angeles and asked the presenter a question on her behalf. The presenter answered it, and I tweeted his response for the person in New Zealand to read. By using Twitter, I had expanded the presenter's reach from the room in Los Angeles all the way to Northern California, Missouri, and New Zealand. When I explained to the presenter what had happened, he said that now he saw how Twitter could be useful and planned to embrace it in upcoming presentations.

Speaker Jared Spool is using the backchannel comments his audiences make during his presentations as a testing ground for his ideas:

> As I finish each presentation, I now go through the Twitterstream to see what folks are saying. At first, it was mostly a vanity play. However, now I'm paying attention to the points they are tweeting and what's not getting any attention. It's changing the way I emphasize the key messages in my presentations.

These are new and interesting rewards that people are finding from using the backchannel that are only possible because of the fundamental ways that Twitter and other social media tools are impacting traditional presentations.

How a Backchannel Changes Presentations

In the backchannel, the small drops that are individual tweets collect to become a powerful Twitterstream that can change information in a presentation from stagnant to flowing and from slow- to fast-moving. As the Twitterstream courses through the backchannel, it is changing the shape of presentations as we know them.

The front channel of a traditional presentation

The traditional mode of presenting is sometimes called *one to many*, meaning that a single presenter delivers information to multiple people in an audience (**Figure 3-1**). This is a popular format that hosts choose for keynotes, lectures, and talks because it is efficient and accepted as the norm.

FIGURE 3-1:
In the traditional model of presentations, information flows from a single presenter to many in the audience.

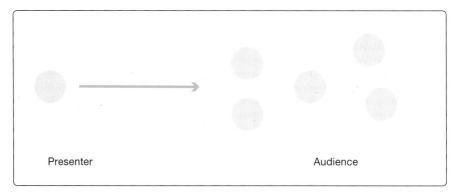

Presenter   Audience

Usually the presenter does most of the talking, and for the most part, the audience sits quietly in their seats looking ahead at the speaker. Audience members don't talk to one another, and may look down at a notepad or laptop to write some notes about the session for their personal use. If their attention wanes, they may daydream, doodle in their notebooks, or stare into space.

In this model, presenters have most of the power to control communication—to speak with power, to persuade with power, and even to use PowerPoint software.

Carving out space for a new conversation

When audiences create a backchannel, they change the traditional arrangement they have with hosts and presenters by carving out a space where they can start a conversation among themselves (**Figure 3-2**), with or without the knowledge of the presenter:

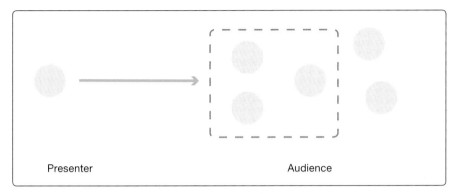

FIGURE 3-2:
The backchannel opens up space for communication among audience members.

Creating a new channel inside the room

As members of the audience begin communicating with one another in the backchannel, suddenly the presenter is no longer the only one talking. A parallel track of communication has now opened up.

Where the presenter is still communicating using a one-to-many model, the audience is communicating using a different many-to-many model as audience members discuss the presentation with one another, as shown in **Figure 3-3**.

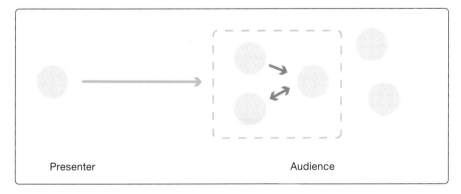

FIGURE 3-3:
The backchannel opens up new communication among audience members.

Usually presenters are not part of this second channel inside the room because they are focusing on what they are saying. Meanwhile in the backchannel, some audience members may focus attention on the speaker as they type notes, some may switch attention between the presenter and the stream of information from other audience members, and some may ignore both the presenter and the backchannel altogether if they're bored.

Creating a new channel outside the room

When people use Twitter for a backchannel, something interesting happens because of the public nature of the service. As described earlier, people on Twitter have their own audiences in the form of their followers, so whenever they post something they open up a new communication channel that extends outside the room (**Figure 3-4**).

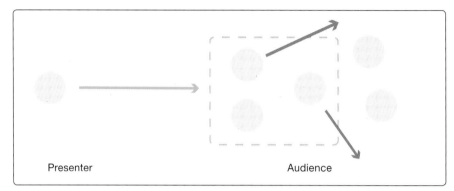

Presenter   Audience

Now anything the presenter says to the people in the room becomes public to people outside the room when an audience member posts the information on Twitter. Anything an audience member says to another audience member becomes public as well. Someone's followers don't have to be following the hashtag from an event to see the posts; they appear with all of the rest of the tweets from the author.

This means that anything leaving a meeting room via a Twitter backchannel has a bigger impact than the same information contained in a traditional presentation room.

The outgoing information has the potential for doing good—for example, when great ideas from a presenter or audience reach a broader audience. And it has the potential for doing harm, as when derisive comments about a speaker are spread far and wide (more on this in Chapter 4).

> **tip ❯** To prevent anyone outside the room from reading what is being written inside the room in the backchannel, some hosts will set up a private, password-protected chat room.

Creating a potentially new channel from back to front, and back

As with any conversation, when audiences discuss a presentation in the backchannel they generate lots of ideas. They often will have questions about what is being said, insights they would like to express, or opinions they would like the presenter to hear and respond to (**Figure 3-5**).

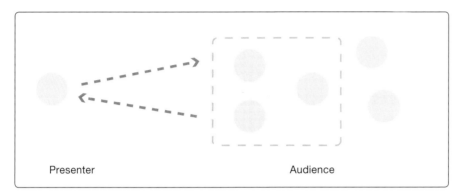

Presenter   Audience

FIGURE 3-5:
The backchannel has the potential to open up a new channel from the back of the room to the front.

But how does the backchannel information get to the presenter? The answer depends on how the host and presenter choose to handle the backchannel.

When hosts and presenters are unaware of what is happening in the backchannel, audiences continue posting their thoughts on Twitter to one another and their followers without interruption. But when hosts and presenters embrace the backchannel, there are a number of things they can do to open up communications with the audience. For example, a host may arrange for a session moderator to monitor the backchannel and assist the presenter; or a presenter might take periodic breaks to scan through the Twitterstream and address any relevant topics. We'll cover a range of practical ways to engage the backchannel in upcoming chapters.

Creating a potentially new channel from outside to front and/or back

The backchannel is so new that it is still a hotbed of experimentation and innovation. For example, when David Pogue asked his followers for a cure for the hiccups and he displayed the results live on the screen, he actually opened up another potential channel of communication—from outside of the room to the front and back (**Figure 3-6** on the next page).

FIGURE 3-6:
The backchannel
can open new
channels, like one
from outside of the
room to the front
and back again.

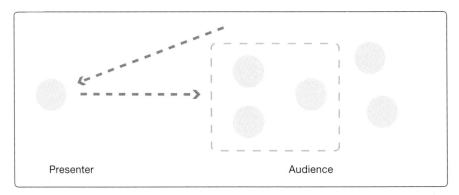

Presenter Audience

David's experiment was on the topic of hiccup cures, and his outside audience was his own Twitter followers, but there are many variations of this you could try yourself. For example, you could ask your audience to ask their own followers for the answer to a question, and then poll your audience for the best ones they collected.

Creating a network conversation

Consultant Nancy White has described the backchannel as a *network conversation,* because in addition to the stream of information flowing from presenter to audience, there are other streams of information flowing among different groups of people both inside and outside the room (**Figure 3-7**).

FIGURE 3-7:
The backchannel
creates a potential
network of
communication
among all those
involved.

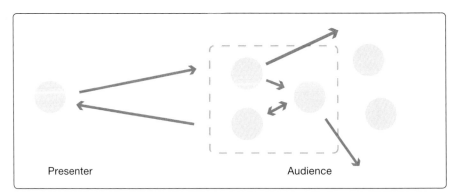

Presenter Audience

The presenter is a major node in the network where the bulk of information originates and flows to others in the room, but at the same time anyone inside or outside of the room can be a node in the network, connecting and conversing with other nodes.

According to Nancy, some of the new realities of the backchannel are

1. Not everybody is paying attention to everything.

2. Not everybody in the network is in the room.

3. You don't even know who is in the network.

4. (It is) not time-bounded.

5. (It is) not place-bounded.

6. (It is) not media-bounded.

Communicating in the backchannel is not a conversation in the sense of a group of people speaking and listening to one another on a single topic. Rather it is a potential network of conversations that can exist among participants inside and outside the room if the participants choose to make it happen. This is not a one-to-many model of communication, nor is it many-to-many; instead it is a hybrid of both.

By opening up new channels of communication as described in this section, the backchannel fundamentally changes the dynamics of presentations, and part of the result is potential rewards—especially for audience members.

The Reward of Engaging Information More Fully

Once a backchannel forms, either unofficially or officially, the Twitterstream begins flowing across audience members' laptops or smart phones, or even on a screen in the room in some cases.

What people do when they participate in a backchannel is as varied as the range of personalities, moods, and roles that people take on at different times.

In many instances, audience members engage information more fully than they otherwise would, by reporting, enhancing, and commenting on it via Twitter (**Figure 3-8** on the next page).

FIGURE 3-8:
The backchannel reports, enhances, and comments on information.

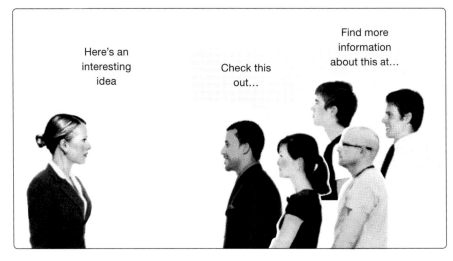

Reporting information

People post the highlights of what's happening in a room and what's being said. They might tweet items like what is shown in **Figure 3-9**.

FIGURE 3-9:
Audiences report information to their followers.

The speaker says business will continue to trend downward a few more months and then it will recover

Top tip from #meeting—focus first on debt ratios

Enhancing information

People will add more facts and support to information they report, such as a link to a website that contains more details. They may share photos using a service like TwitPic, a video using YouTube, or a set of PowerPoint slides using SlideShare. Tweets like this include the example shown in **Figure 3-10**.

FIGURE 3-10:
Audiences enhance information by linking to online resources.

Excellent resource site for marketing tips at http://is.gd

Recent study shows viewership online outpaced offline by 2X—get the full report at http://is.gd

Commenting on information

Sometimes people will add their own opinion to information in the presentation (**Figure 3-11**).

Topic reminds me of a similar theme running through the presentations at the marketing summit

I hadn't thought of things that way— that's a good way to approach the problem at our organization

FIGURE 3-11:
Audiences add additional commentary when they feel it is appropriate.

Some comments are clever or insightful, others are trivial or banal. The best comments are those that add something new or interesting or offer a creative synthesis of ideas.

The Reward of Engaging One Another

By carving out new space for conversations that couldn't exist before, the backchannel opens the way for new dialog among people inside and outside the room (**Figure 3-12**).

This is a new way of thinking about it

I hadn't thought of that

Let's give it a try here

FIGURE 3-12:
The backchannel engages what others are saying, amplifies good points, assists one another, and sometimes arranges to meet in person.

This new conversation carries with it the potential for spreading new ideas, exploring new possibilities, and strengthening community.

People find the backchannel a place to connect and build camaraderie with others in the room who are sharing a common experience. It's a place where people share emotions, such as joy if an event exceeds their expectations.

Monitoring what others saying

Besides publishing their own posts, people in the backchannel search the event hashtag so they can monitor what others are saying about the same experience. That way they can see if they are missing anything or if someone else has a different perspective or insight on the same topic.

Amplifying what others are saying

When someone else in the audience has said something so well that you couldn't say it better, it is common practice to *re-tweet* a post—similar to forwarding an email to your followers. You can recognize a re-tweet because it starts with *RT:* and includes the name of the original author in the post (**Figure 3-13**).

FIGURE 3-13:
Audiences often will
re-tweet someone's
Twitter posts if the
author made a point
better than they did.

RT @speaker1: Top tip from
#meeting—focus on debt ratios

RT @speaker2: Excellent resource site
for marketing tips at http://is.gd

tip ❯ Some third-party Twitter interfaces have built-in re-tweet features that add the formatting automatically at the click of a button.

Helping and meeting one another

Beyond re-tweeting, people connect with other people in the room in a wide range of ways. They may share news about last-minute changes to the schedule, advice about where the best wireless signal strength is, or where to get good coffee (**Figure 3-14**).

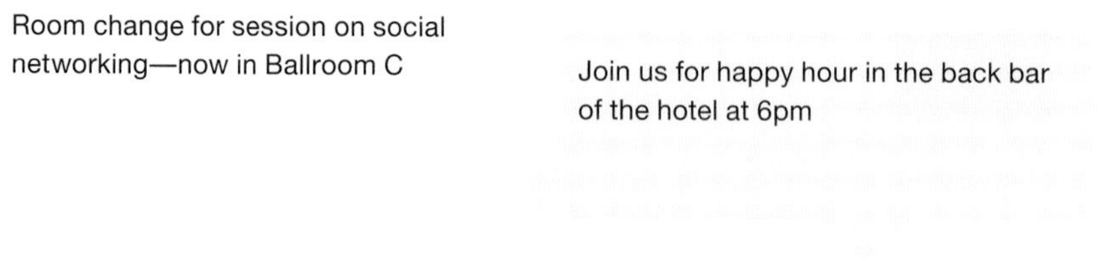

FIGURE 3-14:
Audiences will
help one another
or arrange to meet
in person after a
presentation.

Room change for session on social
networking—now in Ballroom C

Join us for happy hour in the back bar
of the hotel at 6pm

If someone in the audience needs help with something—such as finding a printer or replacing a lost power cord—the backchannel will be sure to help, offering advice, suggestions, and recommendations.

And one of the most useful ways people use the backchannel is to arrange to meet one another in person. This could be a first-time meeting with people who are writing interesting things on Twitter, or it could be a reunion with old friends.

Through the richness as a communications channel, the Twitterstream provides a wealth of opportunities to meet others and have chance encounters with people of mutual interests you otherwise might not meet.

Once a connection is established, Twitter makes it as easy as clicking a button to follow your new and old friends and keep in touch after the event.

> **tip ❯** When people use Twitter to meet in person at a particular place and time, it's called a *tweetup*.

Providing a stage pass for those who cannot be there in person

The people inside the room are not the only ones who can search for a hashtag to view an event's backchannel. Anyone outside the room who is interested in the event can do the same thing. For those people who can't attend the event in person, the backchannel becomes a virtual stage pass to keep them in the loop and connected with their colleagues. People who decided not to attend will often post their regrets that they didn't attend after hearing great feedback in the backchannel.

The Evolution of a Backchannel Twitterer

When people begin using Twitter for the backchannel, they commonly go through phases:

Stage 1: Look what I can do! When the backchannel is new and fun, people are excited about it and write many posts about their first impressions of using the tool.

Stage 2: Here's everything! As people start using the backchannel, they post every detail of everything they hear and see.

Stage 3: Here's the good stuff. As people use the backchannel over time, they post less and carefully screen what they say, often linking to more detailed writeups in longer-form blogs.

Giving new voice to those not comfortable with speaking up

In any audience there are people who simply don't feel comfortable speaking up verbally, but in the backchannel they find a place where they feel more at ease communicating. Sometimes people who rarely say anything in traditional meetings will be some of the most prolific contributors in the backchannel.

Creating options and opportunities

Not everyone in an audience participates in the backchannel, and no one is obligated to participate. If people find topics interesting, they sit back and watch the Twitterstream or jump in and join the conversation. If they find it uninteresting, they will ignore it or just turn off their screen.

At events where the backchannel is a small part of the audience, the feeling is of being part of a tight-knit, in-crowd of the moment. At events of any size, the backchannel interaction between audience members is often clever, funny, enjoyable, and just plain sociable. A lively backchannel can make otherwise slow sessions fun and engaging.

The Reward of More Feedback

In addition to engaging the information and the others in the room, audience members use the backchannel to offer feedback directly to the presenter or host, opening up new lines of communication and dialog and providing the opportunity for clarifying points (**Figure 3-15**).

FIGURE 3-15:
The backchannel asks questions and offers feedback.

Asking questions

During a presentation, people will post questions that ask the presenter to clarify a point or address a point they think is missing (**Figure 3-16**).

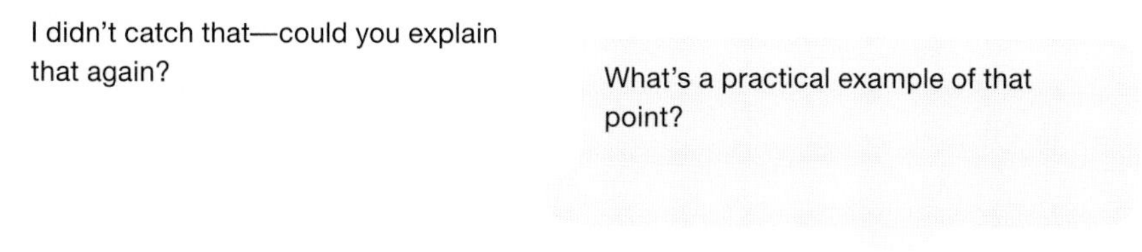

I didn't catch that—could you explain that again?

What's a practical example of that point?

FIGURE 3-16:
If audience members are unclear about a point, they will tweet a question.

Offering compliments and suggestions

Audience members who enjoy a presentation will not hesitate to pass on their thanks and compliments in the backchannel, as well as suggestions for improvement (**Figure 3-17**).

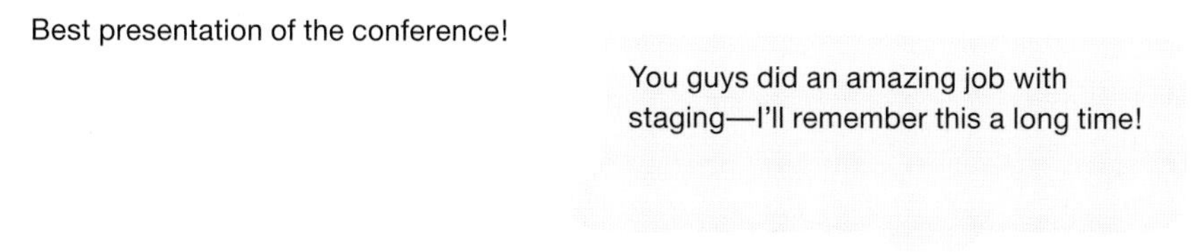

Best presentation of the conference!

You guys did an amazing job with staging—I'll remember this a long time!

FIGURE 3-17:
Audience members will often tweet unsolicited comments about a presentation.

The Reward of Reading the Minds of Audiences

Although it's always been important for presenters to know their audiences, it has been easier said than done. Now, with the backchannel, presenters have more ability than they thought possible to really get to know the people they're speaking to (**Figure 3-18** on the next page).

FIGURE 3-18:
The backchannel
lets hosts and
presenters really
know what's on
the minds of the
audience.

As you scan through any archive of tweets from an active backchannel after a presentation, you'll see a wide range of posts—some useful, some not. But in its aggregate, the archive is a human-filtered body of knowledge representing what was on the mind of those who attended.

Audiences both inside the room and out appreciate its value (**Figure 3-19**).

FIGURE 3-19:
Audiences
appreciate the
value of the
Twitterstream.

I love these Twitter snapshots—thanks
for keeping me posted!

Awesome coverage on Twitter—I didn't
even have to take notes

Through the archived Twitterstream, presenters can find out after the event what the audience thinks of their ideas, research, and delivery. This rich new vein of information has the potential to significantly improve the presentation experience because at last presenters will really know exactly how they did, in real time, unfiltered.

tip ❯ Presenters will find many more benefits from the backchannel, as upcoming chapters will demonstrate.

Diving In to the Backchannel Controversies

People in the backchannel have much to say, and as this chapter described, audiences find tremendous value when they use technology to enhance information, cultivate community, and offer feedback.

But sometimes the feedback an audience has to give is not positive. And when the negative feedback leaves the backchannel and enters the meeting room, it has the potential to provoke confrontations like the one between Whitney and Guy in Chapter 1.

In Chapter 4, we'll jump right in to the fray and examine how backchannels can lead to the risk of some very public blowups.

The Risks
of the
Backchannel

If presenters and audiences aren't prepared
for the impact of a backchannel,
there are risks of misunderstandings
and public blowups

N othing gets attention like conflict, and that's especially true when it comes to the backchannel.

In Chapter 3, you learned that people find the backchannel a very useful tool that helps them to

- More fully engage the information being presented.
- Engage one another.
- Give feedback to the presenter or host.
- Provide a record of audiences' thoughts.

When the feedback the backchannel gives is positive, things go smoothly.

But the waters can get extremely rough when the feedback is negative. In some cases, exchanges between backchannel and presenters have blown up in the room and spilled out into the public square.

When these conflicts happened, the Internet was abuzz with blog posts and comments telling the story and analyzing the play-by-play, often stirring up strong emotions and heated discussions about who was justified in what they did.

The Keyboard vs. the Microphone

The players and the tools these players use to bring about these backchannel blowups are all too common—audience members on their keyboards are pitted against a presenter with a microphone.

It's possible to ignore the backchannel and to just cross fingers and hope that more blowups don't happen. But the risks of doing nothing are actually much greater than having a periodic disruption—they can have big ramifications when they become public.

The Risk of Incivility

At the Les Blogs conference in 2005, Six Apart co-founder Mena Trott delivered a presentation on the topic of civility in blogging. Members of the audience attending the conference—and some outside the room—were using Internet Relay Chat as a backchannel to make comments during Mena's presentation. A large screen on the stage displayed the backchannel comments to the entire audience and to Mena.

After she finished her presentation, Mena took questions from the audience. At one point, Mena glanced over at the screen, read a comment on the backchannel that described her talk as "bullshit" (**Figure 4-1**).

Mena raised her voice and said, "Who is dotBen? All day yesterday you've been an asshole to the people who've been in this panel and I want to know...what the *#$@?"

tip ❯ Watch a video of the interaction between Mena and Ben at the Les Blogs conference at http://www.dltq.org/v1/?p=780.

Ben Metcalfe stood up to acknowledge he was the person who had posted the comment, and explained that he had written it because he thought Mena's talk had been "patronizing." The two had a heated exchange about what Ben had written and whether it was fair for him to be called out in the room for what he had posted to the backchannel.

FIGURE 4-1:
In a widely discussed web video, presenter Mena Trott confronts an audience member over comments he made.

The two agreed to talk about it after the panel. According to posts on their blogs, Ben wrote that "it ended with a smile, a handshake and we even went outside to both cool down and reflect on things," and Mena said, "we were able to spend time talking through these issues in a really productive conversation—including us both apologizing for using such strong words."

But the impact of this backchannel blowup did not end with Mena and Ben's handshake. It continued to reverberate through blog posts and comments as people expressed their opinions of what is appropriate for audiences and presenters to do when the presence of a backchannel somehow disrupts the room.

When the virtual and the real collide

There are differences between what people say in the virtual and often anonymous nature of online communications and what they say to someone face-to-face.

One difference between online and offline conversations is tone. It's common for some people on blogs, discussion forums, and chat rooms to be sarcastic, snarky, or even rude. Part of what fosters this tone is the virtual and often anonymous nature of online conversations: Because people are not saying things directly to other people's faces they may feel freer to take a critical tone. When people in the backchannel go online to make comments, the context may also feel virtual and anonymous. But the reality is that the subject of the comments—the presenter—is there in the room, on occasion reading the comments out loud to everyone.

The juxtaposition of what was meant to be virtual with what has now become face-to-face can be shocking and lead to emotional confrontation.

Assuming privacy

Another difference between online and offline communications is an assumption of privacy. If you're chatting with others in a backchannel, you develop camaraderie and easily assume the conversation will stay among those involved and not reach the presenter.

But the assumed privacy of an online environment does not exist. Again, when the presenter reads backchannel comments out loud, the comments are brought to the attention of everyone in a very public way and whoever made the comments is now publicly accountable for them.

Lacking context

Because of the fast-moving environment that the backchannel creates, and the limited length and context of posts, the environment is ripe for misunderstandings and hurt feelings.

The Risk of Distraction and Confusion

The journal *Nature* reported that at the annual Cold Spring Harbor Biology of Genomes meeting in May 2009, director of meetings and courses David Stewart discovered that audience members were live-blogging scientific information that had not yet been published. This ignited a debate about what information can be blogged or tweeted from scientific conferences and resulted in a policy that anyone who live-blogs or tweets must first seek permission from the speaker.

Part of the discussion about the incident was about whether tweeting contributes to distraction. According to Stewart, "Frankly, it can be a distraction if people are typing on their keyboards in the meeting."

It turns out that the backchannel provides a wealth of opportunities for distraction by audiences, presenters, and hosts.

Distracting speakers

The first thing speakers notice when they present to audiences with a backchannel is that when they stand on stage and look at the audience, not everyone in the audience is looking at them. It's a sign of respect to look at someone when they speak to you, so when speakers see audience members looking at their own individual screens, they can understandably feel that it's rude. Backchannel activity easily distracts a presenter and reduces the eye contact that helps a speaker gauge interest and attention.

It's also distracting for presenters to try to manage what's happening in the backchannel while also presenting. A few talented people can manage the task, but most people struggle with it.

Distracting audience members

It's not only presenters getting distracted—audience members using a backchannel can lose track of what the presenter is saying while they are typing fast to keep up or focusing on reading someone else's post. They also can distract one another with the noise of their typing or the bright screens of smart phones and other gadgets.

Because audience members in the backchannel are connected to the Internet, it's extremely easy for them to be distracted by other online opportunities (such as surfing the web, checking email, and doing other online activities unrelated to the presentation in front of them). That's especially likely to happen if audiences think the material is boring. They simply click to something more interesting online.

The risk of all this distraction is that presenters and audiences are distracted to the point that nobody is focusing on the presentation at hand (**Figure 4-2**).

FIGURE 4-2:
The backchannel can distract both presenters and audiences.

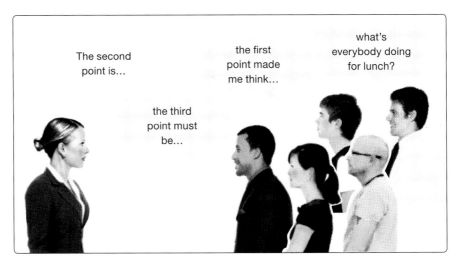

When both presenter and audience are distracted, the quality of the experience plummets for everyone involved. With only partial attention being paid to the presentation, it's easy for anyone to misunderstand someone else, take something out of context, or act based on incomplete information.

The Risk of Unfairness

Another backchannel blowup happened following a presentation at the Canadian Institute Conference on Social Media in Toronto in 2008. Public relations expert and conference co-chair Joseph Thornley had strongly disagreed with some of the points made by former Canadian Broadcasting Corporation producer Ira Basen, and he posted his opinions on Twitter during Ira's talk.

Ira was unaware of Joseph's comments until one of Ira's colleagues sent him a note letting him know about the Twitter posts. Then Ira sent Joseph a strongly worded email:

I guess it's fashionable these days to slag speakers online while they are still on the podium. Why wait until after they are finished so you might have an opportunity to actually reflect on what they had to say? This way, you can impress your friends by how clever you are, as opposed to how insightful. And besides, who has time for reflection in this busy world?

As the blowup ensued, Ira made the point that it's unfair to be criticized live during a presentation without being able to respond. Joseph defended his freedom to make comments during a presentation.

Both Joseph and Ira agreed to post their full email correspondence on Joseph's blog, along with a copy of all of his related Twitter posts from the conference—and he invited people to respond. Readers jumped into the fray in extended posts that became a heated debate on the role Twitter should play as a backchannel tool during live presentations.

Focusing on the presentation, not the backchannel

Presenters normally do not participate in a backchannel because they are focusing on delivering their material. They also may not be involved because they don't even know the audience has created a backchannel. The result is that people in the backchannel are talking about presenters and their material without the presenters taking part in the conversation.

Starting slow

Some presenters may start slow; they might take a while to warm up and find their voice. But backchannel feedback starts when the presentation starts, which means presenters sometimes don't even have a chance to make a point before the backchannel fires off commentary and criticism.

Feeling left out

It's not just presenters who feel the backchannel can be unfair. Other people in the audience who are not participating in the backchannel can feel left out of the conversation, or they find that presenters pay more attention to the backchannel than the live discussion in the room. Some critics accuse people in the backchannel of creating an exclusive club comprised of the "in-crowd."

Letting the few dominate the discussion

A Twitter backchannel wields power because comments are published to the world, but often tweets represent the feedback of only a small, vocal part of the audience— the group that has the strongest opinions but not necessarily the group that reflects the feelings of the larger group. As a result, the backchannel can have disproportionate influence.

If the comments reflect only the opinion of one person, it's unfair to the rest of the audience for the presenter to devote a lot of time to it. And if other people in the audience have their own strong, differing opinions, it's impossible for the presenter to address all of them in the brief time of a presentation.

The Risk of Chaos

Another widely covered backchannel blowup happened in front of a large audience at the South by Southwest Interactive Festival in 2008, where *Business Week* columnist Sarah Lacy was on stage interviewing Facebook CEO Mark Zuckerberg.

During the interview, audience members grew increasingly upset with the manner in which Lacy was conducting the interview. They used the backchannel to express their feelings.

> **tip** ❯ Watch a video of Sarah's interview with Mark at the SXSW 2008 event, and the audience reaction, at http://www.allfacebook.com/2008/03/mark-zuckerberg-sarah-lacy-interview-video/.

In his CNNMoney.com article entitled "Welcome to Conference 2.0: Social media is putting an end to the passive role attendees traditionally play at business conferences," writer Dan Fost described the scene:

Lacy... drew the crowd's wrath by asking Zuckerberg too many questions about his age and his company's outrageous $15 billion valuation and not enough questions about issues more fundamental to how Facebook operates—things like trust, privacy, and accessibility to software developers. On top of that, Lacy interrupted Zuckerberg, seemed to flirt with him, and then grew hostile as the crowd turned against her...

Once again, the blowup didn't end when the session ended. Additional mainstream media covered the fallout and thousands of people viewed online videos of the interview and commented online about the incident. In an effort to better understand what happened, one blogger went so far as to create a minute-by-minute log of the session's Twitter posts and synchronize them with video of the exchange (**Figure 4-3**).

FIGURE 4-3:
In a widely-watched video from the SXSW Interactive Festival in 2008, the backchannel turned against Sarah Lacy during her interview with Facebook CEO Mark Zuckerberg.

The negative taking on a life of its own

As easy as it is to post negative tweets during a live presentation, and to re-tweet them to others, the negativity can quickly snowball in the room. It can reach a point at which it takes on a life of its own, as writer Steven Berlin Johnson describes in his blog:

When enough audience members connect with each other, a consensus room tone can quickly form, with each member's personal outrage amplified silently by his or her neighbors'. Onstage, of course, you see and hear none of this. All you know is that the crowd is quiet until something tips, and they start vocalizing as a group, having been empowered by the backchannel consensus.

Twitter-jacking refers to situations when someone posts a provocative, controversial tweet to get the attention of a room that would otherwise be focused on constructive topics. In these cases, emotion rules over reason—negativity and drama win; positivity and calmness lose.

No one wins with a blowup

Although you can learn something from any situation, when a backchannel blowup happens, nobody wins. The host loses when the audience remembers the bad instead of the good. Presenters lose when the original purpose of a presentation is derailed. And audiences lose when they end up remembering the emotional conflict instead of the information they were there to share.

Understanding Backchannel Blowups

With the ground shifting so quickly and dramatically for presenters and audiences, it's easy to see how conflicts can happen. Someone complains, someone responds in a way that is misread or misunderstood, and sparks fly—igniting an explosion of emotion.

As more audience members create more backchannels, more confrontations are sure to follow. These confrontations can be mitigated—if not altogether averted—by developing a clear understanding of backchannel blowups and their aftermath. Understanding the reasons behind blowups helps hosts, presenters, and audiences understand what they can do to prevent them (or at least what they can do to minimize their impact).

The first place to go to find out why blowups happen is to audiences themselves.

Audiences Are Changing in Fundamental Ways

Is the backchannel a vocal minority or the sign of something bigger happening? If nothing else, the backchannel is a symptom of some key underlying changes among audiences today.

People no longer need to go to presentations to get information

It used to be that live presentations were an important place people would go to get new information. But that has changed with the click of the mouse.

Now people can get the same information from websites, blogs, YouTube, and Twitter, among other sources. With all these places to go for information, audiences don't need to get it from presenters on a stage (**Figure 4-4**).

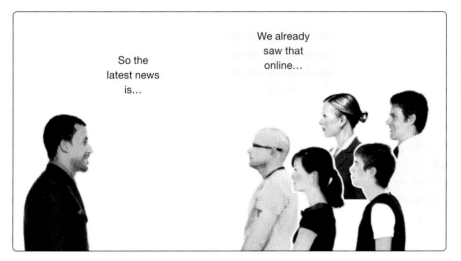

FIGURE 4-4:
Audiences already have access to a great deal of information online, so they are looking for new things from presentations.

When information is readily available elsewhere, audiences start looking for other things they can get from face-to-face meetings. For example, they look for opportunities to collaborate and network.

Audiences have higher expectations

Events expert Jeff Hurt writes in a blog comment that audiences have even higher expectations these days and are more willing than ever to express how they feel:

> *As someone who plans education events, hires presenters, and culls through presentation evaluation data, I'm finding that my attendees are becoming less tolerant of speakers that do not provide relevant, current, and timely content. Attendees' written comments have become more critical of speakers than I've ever seen in the past 15+ years. I speculate it's because attendees view their time and attention as their resources, equivalent to money. They don't want to waste their time, their attention, or their money.*

This means audiences no longer tolerate boring PowerPoint presentations (**Figure 4-5**).

Instead, audiences today demand information they can't get elsewhere, along with compelling graphics and engaging multimedia. Audiences now insist presenters get to the point, speak clearly, and avoid corporate-speak. They want presentation experiences to be human and authentic, not impersonal, overly slick, or based on a one-size-fits-all PowerPoint template.

FIGURE 4-5:
Audiences have grown frustrated after years of enduring presentations in which presenters simply read the bullet points from their slides.

Though audiences today say they don't like PowerPoint loaded with bullet points, they do still like visuals. The quality of the visual material you choose to present needs to be as good as what your audience is accustomed to seeing on an everyday basis. This expectation will continue to raise the bar on the quality of presentations from keynote-level speakers. At the same time, the trend toward more audience-driven experiences reduces demand for professional lecturers and increases demand for professional facilitators.

Audiences want more participation

One of the core questions audiences are asking today is: When is *presentation* (the one-way delivery of information) the best fit and when is *conversation* (the two-way exchange of information) the best fit.

The traditional lecture format is biased toward a particular subset of an audience that can learn by sitting quietly and listening. But most audiences today simply don't want to sit quietly as passive vessels receiving wisdom from a speaker upon high (**Figure 4-6**). Instead they expect to be more involved as active participants, helping to create the experience.

FIGURE 4-6:
Most audiences no
longer sit still.

The general trend is for audiences to turn the dial from presentation to conversation, from passive reception to active engagement, and from speaker-driven to audience-driven formats. As audiences become active participants, they want more of a say in determining the agenda. They influence meetings from the preplanned toward the spontaneous, from the linear to the modular—and they want a say in the matter.

> **tip** ❯ Chapter 7 describes practical ways to make your presentations more conversational.

There are many situations in which a speaker-driven model is appropriate, but there is a rapidly increasing number of situations where this model is no longer a good fit. Hosts are tasked with the ever-important challenge of finding the right position on the dial between presentations and conversations.

Audiences will vote with their feet if they don't find what they want

With so many options available, audiences are no longer willing to tolerate situations where they feel their time is being wasted. And why should they?

Rather than sit in the audience and take it, they're now either surfing for more interesting topics on the web or simply walking out of the room altogether (**Figure 4-7** on the next page).

FIGURE 4-7:
Audiences simply leave a presentation if they feel it wastes their time.

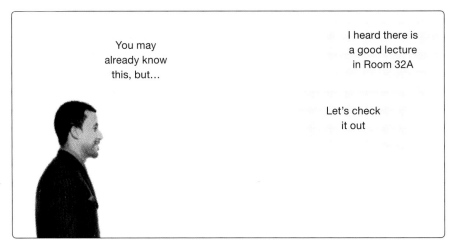

Many of these changing audience expectations are related to an important trend in meetings called Open Space.

Opening Up to Change in Presentation Approaches

In his book *Open Space Technology: A User's Guide*, Harrison Owen describes a situation in which 225 people meet to hash out an agreement on how to spend $1.5 billion for highway construction across public and tribal lands. The participants—one-third Native Americans, one-third federal government officials, and one-third state and local government officials—were historically at odds with one another. Few in the group expected an amicable resolution.

An even more daunting challenge? There was purposely no meeting agenda and no presentations scheduled for the two days set aside for the meeting.

But in short order, the group managed to get significant work done, according to Harrison:

> *The agenda itself was created in less than half an hour, and the various task groups produced about 150 pages of proceedings in 36 hours...and copies...rolled hot off the press in time for the departure of all participants on the morning of the third day. During the concluding session, one of the Native Americans said that never before had he felt so listened to and so much a part of the discussion. The feeling was shared by all parties.*

Harrison had introduced Open Space Technology to the group. In the 25 years since he developed Open Space, Harrison reports that more than 200,000 meetings in 124 countries have used the approach for an astonishing range of purposes—from budget allocation to architectural planning to peace talks in the Middle East.

But how can any specific meeting approach help groups around the world accomplish so much, especially when there is no preplanned agenda, no prepared speeches, and no idea in advance how anything will get done?

> **tip ❯** See Web Appendix D at www.backchannelbook.com for a detailed description of how Open Space meetings work and how dramatically different the approach is from traditional meetings.

If you have not experienced an Open Space meeting (**Figure 4-8**), the concept seems unbelievable and no description will do it justice. People who hear about the concept are skeptical, and the only thing that changes their opinions is actually participating in such an event in person.

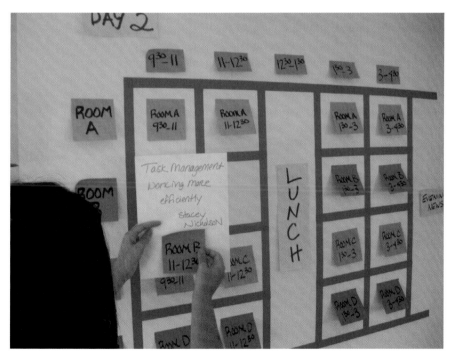

FIGURE 4-8: Open Space Technology is a fundamentally different way of conducting meetings that is influencing events around the world.

As described in detail in Web Appendix D, the Open Space approach introduces self-organizing principles and techniques that give audiences full responsibility for every aspect of meetings. One of the most influential ideas to come from Open Space is the *Law of Two Feet* (also known as the *Law of Mobility*), which states:

> *If, during our time together, you find yourself in any situation where you are neither learning nor contributing, use your two feet and go to some more productive place.*

Walking through the halls of conferences (such as the South by Southwest Interactive Festival), it's very common to see attendees using the Law of Two Feet. If they are not satisfied with a presentation, they leave. Then they describe in the backchannel why they weren't satisfied. Or they walk in to a presentation once it's underway based on good comments they heard through the backchannel.

A bigger movement toward opening up more space

According to trends and events throughout the world, it looks like we need to buckle our seat belts for more involvement like the kind inspired by Open Space.

In a Weber Shandwick study released in early 2009, major event organizers indicated they are ramping up for more audience engagement and involvement:

> *...conference organizers reported they are planning more time for Q&A (72% more vs. three years ago), more interactive sessions between speaker and audience (70%), and more panel sessions (64%). They are planning fewer keynote sessions (30%) than they did three years ago.*

There is, indeed, a thirst for more involvement that hosts are aiming to quench. At some conferences and gatherings, the change is already well underway.

A conventional conference opens itself up

A few years ago, the organizers of the National Educational Computing Conference (NECC) noted that their attendance numbers were down. They needed to do a radical rethink of how they created an experience that their 20,000 attendees were willing to pay to attend.

Donella Evoniuk, senior director of conference services, had heard about Open Space and also had observed how often people were using online social networking tools to create community and collaborate around ideas. She also noticed a new trend people really liked on the massive exhibit hall floor: mini theaters with product demonstrations, where they could get up after a few minutes and go on to the next one.

Seeing the big trends in participation underway, NECC organizers made a dramatic break from the traditional PowerPoint model and turned the conference programming upside down. In 2007, they took 65 percent of the content that was previously shared in meetings and put it in the public spaces in an interactive format (including technology playgrounds, cafés, and working sessions). There were still traditional keynotes and panels, but the focus was now on freeing up people to either direct their own learning or to learn from one another.

The response was phenomenal. Attendee Kristin Hokanson expressed this sentiment in a blog post describing her experience at NECC in 2009:

> The real learning at this conference isn't going on behind closed doors, seated in rows, with the speaker in the front shuffling their PowerPoints—showing and telling. It is in places where people can get together in small groups share, converse, and experiment.

Though the NECC organizers didn't specifically use Open Space techniques, they did use them in spirit. "The thinking that (Open Space) provided to look at things differently was huge," Donella said. After hearing about it, she remembers thinking about the conventional approach to meetings, "Wow—we don't have to do it this way!"

Unconferences and camps

Some audiences aren't even waiting on event hosts to create a more interactive experience; these audiences are already organizing their own events instead. This is especially true in the technology industry, where Open Space has influenced many events and meetings, particularly camps and unconferences.

The *camp* movement began as an invitation-only gathering of about 200 tech experts who pitched tents outside the offices of O'Reilly Media in Sebastopol, California. Inspired by Open Space, the group created their own agenda and ran their own sessions over a weekend—and they did so to rave reviews by attendees.

Soon a spinoff known as BarCamp opened its events to anyone who wanted to attend and at any location where a host wanted to sponsor one. The camp movement has since exploded in popularity (**Figure 4-9**). For example, it includes events covering specialized technical topics (such as WordCamp), events for people working with open-source technology (such as WordPress), and events for podcasters and social media practitioners (such as PodCamp). Camps now gather around a range of professions and topics, including ProductCamp for marketers and product managers, EduCamp for those in education, and even LaidOffCamp for recently unemployed people or solo entrepreneurs.

FIGURE 4-9:
The BarCamp website features hundreds of camps held in locations all over the world.

USA

1. Jan 10th, 2009 - BarCampHarrisburg Harrisburg, PA
2. Jan 17th, 2009 - DesignCamp - Bryan/College Station, TX
3. Jan 20th, 209 - CloudCampAtlanta - Atlanta, GA
4. Jan 23rd 2009 BarCampCharlotte - Charlotte,NC
5. Jan 24th, 2009 - ProductCamp Austin Winter 2009 - Austin, TX
6. Jan 24, 2009 - PhotoCampHouston - Houston, TX
7. Jan 24, 2009 - NewsInnovation UM - Columbia, MO
8. Jan 24th, 2009 - NewsInnovation DC - Washington DC
9. Jan 31st, 2009 - FreelanceCampSanAntonio (www.barcamp.org/freelancecampsatx) - San Antonio, TX
10. Feb 7th, 2009 - AtlantaSkeptiCamp - Atlanta, GA
11. Feb 11th, 2009 - HomelessConnectCamp - San Francisco, CA
12. Feb 20-22, 2009 - RecentChangesCamp - Portland, OR
13. Feb 21st, 2009 - AccessCampSanAntonio - San Antonio, TX
14. February 22, 2009 - BarCampMiami 2009 Adrienne Arsht Center for the Performing Arts in downtown Miami, Florida.
15. Coming Early 2009 - BarCampBankMadison - Madison, WI
16. February 27, 2009 - HealthCampDc - Washington DC. Part of the HealthCamp series of events.
17. February 28, 2009 - ProductCampBoston - Boston, MA
18. February 28, 2009 - PresentationCamp - Stanford, CA
19. February 28, 2009 - CloudCampSeattle - Seattle, WA
20. February 28 - March 1st - TransparencyCamp - Washington, DC
21. March 3, 2009 - LaidOffCamp - San Francisco, CA
22. March 3, 2009 - BarCampBuffalo - Buffalo, NY
23. March 6-7, 2009 - BarCampMoneyNYC 2009 - New York, NY.
24. March 7, 2009 - SocialCampMemphis - Memphis, TN

The term *unconference* refers to any loosely structured gathering that is distinguished from a formally organized conference (such as BloggerCon, an early unconference for bloggers). Kaliya Hamlin, a consultant who has designed and facilitated more than 100 unconferences in the tech industry over the past five years, describes an unconference as "more organized than a cocktail party and less organized than the talking heads on a panel (discussion)."

Kaliya uses Open Space as the basis for 80 percent of the events she facilitates; she applies a blend of other approaches as she deems appropriate to the other 20 percent of events. Because unconferences are so much cheaper to produce, and they create such high levels of participant satisfaction, Kaliya describes them as 10 times cheaper and 10 times better than traditional conferences.

The impact of Open Space on the backchannel

In looking at the backchannel through the eyes of audiences who have attended Open Space events, camps, and unconferences, you gain a better understanding of why some people create alternate communication channels in the first place. They feel excluded or unhappy with the presentation format and they want something different (even though they may not yet know what it is).

Many early adopters of the backchannel have experienced Open Space principles in action, and when they return to speaker-driven meetings, they are often dissatisfied because traditional formats simply don't deliver the same quality of experience.

Open Space is definitely an important part of the evolving presentation mix—it's influencing current events and audiences, and it's part of the bigger trend toward more participation. It simply has to be put on the table when you get ready to engage the backchannel.

Maximizing the Rewards, Minimizing the Risks

The backchannel introduces the opportunity for reward and risk for both presenters and audiences. Whichever result it creates will depend on how each party engages the changes that are afoot.

Embracing the change

The most important thing hosts, presenters and audiences can do is to fully understand the changes that are impacting traditional presentations. These include many of the issues described in this chapter and the previous chapter:

- The changing dynamics that the backchannel introduces.
- The changing expectations of audiences.
- The external forces (such as Open Space) that are influencing the way traditional events and meetings are conducted.

Coming to a new agreement

As more audiences use Twitter and other tools to create backchannels, and as presenters learn how to engage them, all parties must come to a new agreement.

For example, a simple code of conduct for audiences to use when they tweet during live presentations would go a long ways toward reducing the risk of the backchannel blowups described in this chapter.

Audience Guidelines for Backchannel Feedback

Audiences should follow these simple guidelines to help prevent backchannel blowups:

- Tweet unto others as you would have them Tweet unto you.
- Be accurate.
- Say something good before you say something bad.
- Stay aware of your Twitterstream reputation.

See Web Appendix C for a more detailed description of a proposed backchannel agreement among hosts, presenters, and audiences.

By examining the risks and renegotiating the current contract between all the parties involved in a presentation, we can reduce risks and expand our potential rewards.

If you're interested in taking part in negotiating a new agreement, see Web Appendix C at www.backchannelbook.com, which includes a draft of a backchannel agreement among hosts, audiences, and presenters. Or join the conversation about the agreement at www.backchannelbook.com.

Getting practical

Finally, there are the practical things speakers can do to engage the backchannel. The rest of this book focuses on these things you can do to prepare yourself for the new world of presenting that awaits you.

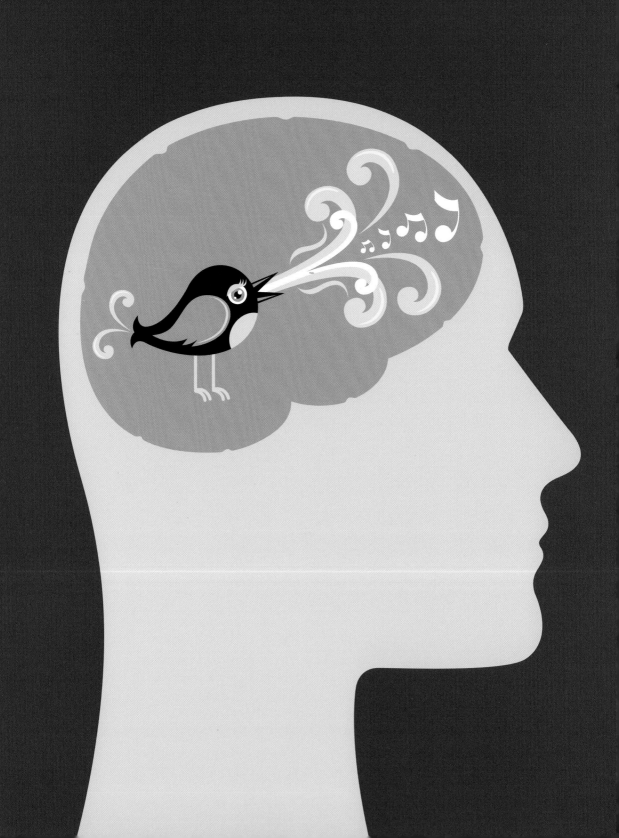

Preparing for the Backchannel

Make more space for a bigger conversation
with a backchannel by taking a
longer-term view of presentations and shifting
more of your content online

R eady or not, the new world of the backchannel has arrived.

When you stand in front of your next audience, you face a group of people who you're lucky to be seeing. In an ever-increasingly attention-deprived world, they have taken time out of their schedules to focus their attention on your topic.

You have what has long been a presenter's dream: a way to peer into your audience's minds and to get instant feedback through the backchannel. And when you reach them, your audiences have laptops and smartphones at the ready to engage your ideas and spread them far and wide into the world.

So if you're a presenter or a host, what can you do to make the most of it? What exactly do you do to embrace, encourage, and facilitate the backchannel?

Affirming What Doesn't Change

As much as the backchannel is changing audiences (**Figure 5-1**), you can rest assured there's still a great deal that does not change. The classic elements that make up a good presentation remain the bedrock of effective communications.

There are plenty of excellent books, courses, and programs that can help you develop the fundamentals that you'll always need to know to communicate effectively, no matter what the context.

Being a good presenter has always been about knowing who you are, your strengths and weaknesses, and the set of skills that help you communicate effectively. When you are knowledgeable about your topic, passionate about it, and authentic to your person and personality, you'll do a good job. Knowing yourself and integrating who you are with your public performance give you a sense of authenticity and confidence that resonate with audiences.

As always, you should be clear about why you are giving a presentation in the first place. That's especially true these days, when a meeting certainly is not the most efficient way to send information. Picking up the phone, writing an email, typing an

FIGURE 5-1: Presenting to an audience with a backchannel may look different, but many of the classic techniques of public speaking still apply.

instant message, or sending a report will often do the trick. A meeting should be a last resort, used only after you've ruled out other ways to get information across.

A meeting can be an efficient way to help people learn something new that they otherwise couldn't learn on their own. Or it can serve to explain difficult information, to prioritize, to persuade, to make a decision, and to come to consensus.

A good presentation has always been about the audience; it's not about the presenters and their performances. The better you know your audience, the better you can tailor your presentation to their needs. When you serve an audience well, you help them learn and take something away that they can use.

And you've always been able to use tools and technologies at your disposal to help you get your point across. These days, they include flip charts, projectors and screens, presentation software, audience response systems, and now, social media and the backchannel.

Surveying the New Landscape of the Backchannel

Although the backchannel is a new phenomenon, don't be overwhelmed by the prospect of engaging it.

If you've been a public speaker for a while, you have to adjust your game. If you've just started giving presentations, you have tremendous potential to become an even better presenter when you engage the changes the backchannel introduces.

Assuming the best

The best way to start thinking about the backchannel is to be positive about the opportunity before you. Your audience is not your enemy. They are the same people they have always been, except now they are using new tools.

It may be disconcerting at first to look at your audience and find that they are looking down at their laptops or smartphones (**Figure 5-2**). Just assume they are taking notes, writing down questions they have for you, and extending your ideas well out into the world.

FIGURE 5-2: Assume that your audience members who are on laptops and smartphones are talking about your ideas and spreading them out into the world.

You can't control or even manage the backchannel, but you can engage, nurture, and influence the people who use it—and by doing that, you persuade them to be powerful advocates for spreading your ideas.

Reaching out

By reaching out to those in your audience who are in the backchannel, you are making an effort to recognize them. People in the backchannel are an important subset of your audience because of their ability to reach and influence others.

When you make an explicit effort to connect with the backchannel, you make a statement that you are aware of and engaged in current events, activities, and trends. You let them know that you're on board with the notion of using the latest tools and techniques to reach your audience more effectively.

Learning new skills

You already may have strengths that play well to the backchannel. For example, those well-suited for presenting to the backchannel have the capacity to monitor multiple streams of information and quickly make adjustments according to what is happening. If you're one of those lucky people, you're in a great position to manage the many things happening during a backchannel presentation.

That doesn't mean that the rest of us can't learn the new skills it takes to present to these new audiences. If you're among this latter crowd, you'll just need to do more planning and practicing to make sure you've covered the essentials you need to have for your new presentations.

In addition to the classic speaking skills mentioned earlier, you now have to

- Become familiar with social media technologies like Twitter and how your audiences use them.
- Use new online research tools and techniques to find out more about your audience before presentations.
- Learn how to engage the backchannel before, during, and after presentations.

You learned how to join a Twitter backchannel in Chapter 2. Now you need only to learn the techniques and tools covered in the rest of this book to become more familiar with these new skills. You don't need to master them; some basic familiarity will do.

Promoting four "wants" to "needs"

Presentations have always involved a few key areas:

- **Planning:** How you will accomplish your objectives.
- **Content:** What you will say.
- **Engagement:** How your audience will be able participate.
- **Delivery:** What you do when you actually stand before your audience on the day of the presentation.

As a presenter you've probably always wanted to plan a full strategy for your ideas, make the content easier to understand, engage your audience, and stay flexible in your delivery.

But now the backchannel is turning these "wants" into "needs" as audiences demand new ways of engaging you and your information:

- **Fully planning for your audience:** You've always had to plan for your audience, but planning for a backchannel audience demands new approaches. This chapter covers new ways to expand and extend your thinking on how to present your ideas both online and offline.

- **Making your ideas easier to digest:** It's always been important to express your ideas in a way that makes them easy for an audience to digest, understand, and pass along. But now audiences want you to get to the point even faster, so you have to work harder to distill your ideas and express them in ways that are Twitter-friendly. Chapter 6 shows you how to do this.

- **Involving your audience even more:** Audiences simply are no longer passive and instead want to be an active part of a conversation with you. In Chapter 7, you learn a range of techniques to help you to involve your audience.

- **Improvising your delivery even more:** The day of the formal, preplanned presentation is nearing an end. In a live environment, you will need to adjust your material to your audiences, keep a positive tone, neutralize negativity, and be ready to handle hecklers both in the room and online. In Chapters 8 and 9, you learn practical ways to hold together the fast-moving backchannel environment.

With these new skills in place, you'll be ready to engage the backchannel at your next presentation.

Of course, the best place to get started is at the beginning—the way you approach your presentation when you start thinking about it.

Starting an Even Bigger Conversation

Because of the many ways the backchannel changes the way audiences engage information, you'll need to step back and look at the basis for how you view your presentations.

Viewing a presentation as a one-time event

It's not uncommon today to view a presentation as a one-time event that occurs within a finite span of time. From a presenter's perspective, you prepare to stand on stage, deliver your materials, and when the applause dies down, it's done.

From an audience's perspective (**Figure 5-3**), they attend the event, maybe ask a question during Q&A, fill out a questionnaire, and, in some cases, they get a copy of the slides you delivered. At that point, it's pretty much all over.

FIGURE 5-3:
It's common to view a presentation as a one-time event with limited opportunities for interaction.

But in the era of the backchannel, the notion of a one-time interaction is gone.

Expanding your view to a long-term relationship

As described in previous chapters, your audience members in the backchannel are online during your presentations and can access a lot of information in a variety of ways, so it reduces the need for you to make a presentation an *information-transfer* experience. You can instead make it a *relationship-building* experience.

Instead of looking at any group of people who attend a presentation as a monolithic "audience," look at them as people you are developing relationships with. Via the backchannel, you can cultivate existing audiences who are interested in you and your ideas, sign up new audience members, and reach out to people you have yet to meet.

As you create a flow of communication over time, the various points when and where you contact people—via newsletter, blog post, Twitter, and so on—become opportunities to grow relationships (**Figure 5-4**). In this context, live presentations are special events that can enhance relationships through in-person interaction.

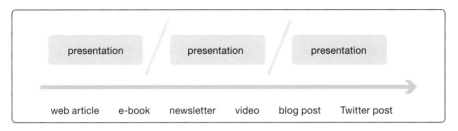

FIGURE 5-4:
When you take a longer-term view, live presentations are only one of the many ways you engage people over time.

As you shift focus from the short-term, one-time events to long-term, ongoing relationships with your audience members, you'll build trust and a community of people committed to you, your ideas, and your ability to make a positive difference in their lives.

Attracting Twitter followers

This long-term relationship view dovetails with a long-term strategy of attracting followers on Twitter over time. As described in Chapter 2, if you're a public speaker, it's in your best interest to grow a base of Twitter followers who are interested in you and your ideas. You can do this by actively publicizing your Twitter address in all of your communications and by tweeting on a regular basis on topics your followers find useful, interesting, or insightful.

Over time, you'll build a community of Twitter followers who can help you in many ways, such as by giving you feedback on ideas, researching topics, and providing case studies. Ideally you may eventually have followers who are also members of your live audiences, providing you with valuable allies you can connect with during your presentations.

Getting your audience to know you before you stand on stage

Cultivating relationships over time creates a bigger context and friendlier tone to your live presentations because your audiences will know something about you and your ideas before you even begin speaking. The more your audience knows about you and your ideas before you step on stage, the better.

You'll also need to reach out to the segment of your audience that is not physically in the room, but rather is attending your presentation virtually through the backchannel. If you look at this group within a long-term relationship strategy, you'll make extra effort to recognize them and make them feel as welcomed, included, and informed as the people who are there in the chairs. Chapter 7 will show you ways you can do this.

But if you give people who are not there a similar quality experience as those who are there, might you diminish the reasons for people to come in the first place? Maybe for a small number of people, but when most people who couldn't be there see what they missed, they'll make that much more effort to attend in person the next time they are able.

Re-centering your presentation universe

Just as the backchannel changes how you look at a presentation
in time, it also changes the way you look at it in terms of informational space.

Everyone has a story to tell, but these days you have to find more ways than ever to tell it. Your "big story" is the message you have to offer that people find meaningful.

Your live presentation is only one slice of a very big communications pie that offers your tasty story to a hungry audience (**Figure 5-5**).

FIGURE 5-5:
Your live presentation is only one slice of your big story.

Live
presentation

Big
Story

When you shift the center of your universe from the live presentation to the big story itself, you open up new ways of looking at the full range of ways you communicate your message.

Writing once, publishing many

You've always had multiple ways to get your message across besides a live presentation. But a presentation in particular has always taken a disproportionate amount of time, effort, and emotion to create. If you put that much work into preparing and delivering a presentation, why not put that effort to its broadest possible use?

A presentation is not the only time you say something, nor the only time you will need to say it. Since people now get their information in an endless variety of places, you have to find ways to tell your story in different formats where people are paying attention. That means extending your thinking from a PowerPoint presentation all the way out to the different places where your audiences are.

This approach helps your audiences to easily and efficiently get your core information in a range of different places before, during, and after your presentation.

Telling your story across a range of media offers your audiences many more ways to engage your information beyond your live presentation, creating a much bigger scope and reach for your ideas.

For example, in addition to your live presentation you may tell your single story using

- Your website.
- Your blog.
- Email.
- YouTube—the popular video sharing service.
- SlideShare—a presentation sharing service similar to YouTube.
- Twitter.

In this new view, your big story is the center of the communications universe, and a live presentation is only one of many ways you can communicate your message (**Figure 5-6** on the next page). You focus on your big story in the center first and then work outward to create ways to get the word out in many different formats—an important one being the live, in-person presentation.

FIGURE 5-6:
When you tell your
single big story
outward through
multiple media, you
spread the fruit of
your presentation
labor across more
places to reach
people wherever
they are.

When you shape your big story in its many forms, you give people a mission they can rally around and you provide them with a way to act on their new enthusiasm.

In whatever medium you present your ideas, be sure to package them in a way that makes it easy for people to spread them. For example, the TED Conference records live presenters and offers links to the videos for free. People can easily share the links to the videos by email, Facebook, or other social media, extending the ideas long after the presentation ended to audiences bigger than the presenter would have thought possible.

Extending the conversation along across the multiple platforms

A major benefit of expanding the time and space of your thinking about presentations is that as you create a range of formats for your ideas, you're also creating many more opportunities to engage people in conversation.

Any conversational touch point is an opportunity to get feedback on your ideas, and by beginning this process early, you fine-tune your concepts early and often.

Creating a Presentation Home Page

As described previously in this chapter, one of the significant new changes the back-channel introduces to presentations is the ability for audience members to be connected to the Internet during your presentations.

When people in the backchannel go looking for your ideas in the many places they reside—websites, blogs, Twitter, and more—they likely find only fragments of your ideas (not the whole story).

By providing a single location for the depth of what you have to say, you bring a sense of coherence to what could otherwise be a disjointed experience.

Creating a community place

To provide a single place where you and the backchannel can build an online home together, create a simple web page where everyone can go. In the next section we'll look at a fast and easy way to do this.

The focus of this single page is your big story and related resources—one-stop shopping for your ideas in their multiple formats (**Figure 5-7**).

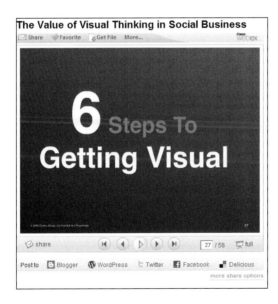

FIGURE 5-7:
Services such as SlideShare are starting to give you ways to centralize your presentation resources in a single area online.
(Example slides by David Armano)

Backchannels are usually are set up by audience members who create temporary community areas that are not integrated into the actual presentation experience in any meaningful way. Because they are not integrated with the presentation or presenter, they're disconnected and often disappear after the event.

Your challenge is to more effectively organize the experience by using a simple web page to create synergy between the backchannel and the actual experience in the room. This creates a home for everyone, including those inside the room and those outside the room (following the event via the backchannel).

When everyone—both inside the room and out—has a common place to go online, you create synergy, context, and community around your ideas.

Shifting out of PowerPoint to make more room for conversation offline

Though the time allowed for live presentations is limited, there's a general tendency to pack as much information as possible into a presentation. The school of thought is that if you say and show more, your audience will take away more. But your audience members are limited in their capacity to process new information, so they retain only a relatively small amount of information within the limited time of a presentation.

With a presentation home page, you can actually ease your worries about getting all of the information to your audience. To do this, start building your presentation online, rather than in PowerPoint.

As you begin to assemble your presentation, put the bulk of your material on your presentation home page, including all the detail and source materials you have. For example, if you are a marketing executive presenting a set of recommendations to a decision-making team, place all related materials online, such as

- A copy of your presentation file.
- Spreadsheets you used to analyze market research data.
- Links to videos of customers you interviewed.
- Case studies that demonstrate your ideas in action.
- A bibliography of resources you used.

Making all of this detail available online helps you avoid overload that happens when you try to present more information than the audience can handle.

When you're secure your audience can find any depth of information they need through links to the online resources, focus next on creating simple slides that cover only the most important information you want to communicate (more on this in Chapter 6).

When you reach a point in your presentation when you refer to detailed informa-tion, tell your audience that you have created a presentation home page where you have placed all of the detail that supports your point. Use an URL shortener to create a simple link to your page and provide it verbally, on your slides, and on any printed materials you have handed out.

By providing an online location for your background information, you offer those in the backchannel the opportunity to explore details if they wish. And by keeping the detail off of your slides, your audience can focus on the fewer, more important ideas on your slides. This creates more time for your audience to get involved, connect, and even learn from one another during the actual presentation.

> **tip ❯** Because people in the backchannel are reporting live on your presentation, everything you say is now on the record; and because your audience is online, they're likely checking your facts. Make your audiences' research easier by citing your sources on your presentation home page and letting them know they can find further information there.

Setting Up a Presentation Wiki as a Simple Start

It's easy to create a simple web page where you put all the resources related to your presentation. It can be as simple as adding a new page to your website, setting aside a new area on your blog, or creating a new page on a wiki.

A *wiki* is a tool you can use to create a web page that others can access and add or edit content. Search the web for the word *wiki* and you'll find a range of services that range from free to paid, for individual users or corporate teams. The technology itself encour-ages your audience members to get involved with the material, much in the same spirit they get involved with the backchannel; for example, they can easily add new resources, links, or even videos. (If you're not comfortable providing that much control or interac-tion, use a traditional web page or blog area that only you can access.)

If you build your presentation home page using a wiki, it's easiest to start with a single page. As you add more materials, you may add more pages along with navigation links to access them.

To begin building your presentation wiki, sign up for an account with a wiki hosting service. Set up a single page and add a few headings, such as

- Event details.
- Session description.
- Bio and contact information.
- Presentation slides.
- Source materials.
- Handouts.
- Feedback.

After you have the headings in place (**Figure 5-8**), add a brief description or a link to the corresponding resources.

FIGURE 5-8:
Begin the backchannel presentation creation process by creating a wiki page for your presentation. This one was created using a free account at PBworks.com.

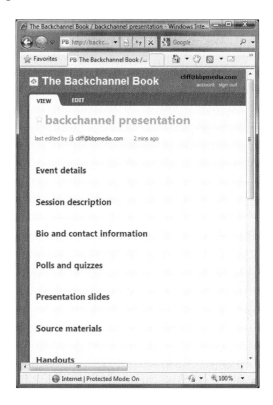

The new wiki page you built has a unique URL you can now share with your audiences when you deliver your presentation.

Adding More Material to Your Presentation Home Page

Adding a few text headings on a one-page wiki is a simple way to create a presentation home page to get started. Whatever tool you use, consider adding a range of resources to your home page to create a robust community area for your presentation (**Figure 5-9**).

FIGURE 5-9:
Your presentation home page should aggregate the various ways people can interact with your idea and provide them with the ability to easily share the ideas in whatever form and context they prefer.

The following section provides samples of material you can add to your presentation home page.

Moving beyond the basics

The example of the presentation wiki in the previous section included some of the basics you should include in a presentation home page, such as your presentation description, contact information, your source materials, and copies of your slides. In addition to these basics, consider adding additional material to make the presentation home page even more useful and dynamic.

Uploading your handouts

One of the great presentation questions is, "When is it appropriate to provide hand-outs to my audience?" Some audience members like to have something they can write notes on. Yet some speakers hesitate to provide handouts because audience members may become distracted by reading the handouts instead of paying attention to the presentation. And some audiences and speakers alike complain of the environmental waste of printing handouts that only get thrown in the trash afterward.

The best thing to do in the age of the backchannel is to upload an electronic version of your handouts to your presentation home page, announce their location to your audience, and let them decide what to do. The approach may not satisfy those who want printouts in their hands during the presentation, but at least everyone will have an electronic version as a record of what you said (and they can print them later if they wish).

Embedding videos

Your presentation home page is a good place to embed any videos you have that are related to the material you're presenting. For example, if you have a brief YouTube video describing some aspect of the ideas in your presentation, embed the link to the video here so audience members can easily share the material with others.

> **tip ⟩** Share your own examples of your presentation home pages by adding a link to the wiki at www.backchannelbook.com.

Listing attendees

A big benefit of the backchannel is that it offers the opportunity for people in the audi-ence to connect with other people of common interests.

To make it even easier for people to connect, you can add the attendee list from the event registration form to the presentation home page (so long as you've received permission from attendees beforehand).

And to further maximize this opportunity, invite people in the backchannel who are not in the room to add their contact information to the presentation home page (it's easy for people to do this if you've used a wiki) so others in the room can contact them.

Embedding a live video feed of the presentation

In addition to the basics, consider adding resources to your presentation home page such as live video; it's probably not as difficult to do this as you might think.

A live video feed of your presentation is a very powerful way to spread your ideas. For people inside the room, the feed is multimedia documentation of what you are saying. For people outside the room, you have created a powerful way for them to see you in action.

> **tip** ❯ As mentioned in Chapter 2, web tools are evolving rapidly—be sure to visit the wiki at www.backchannelbook.com to see the latest that readers recommend.

To set up a live video feed, you'll need to arrange for someone to set up a video camera to capture your talk. Larger conferences often provide a professional video team to record an event, but these days the technology is simple enough that you can do it yourself or with the help of some of your audience members.

Once you've set up the camera, plug it into the USB port of a computer and then set up a service such as Ustream.tv (**Figure 5-10**) or Livestream to receive the feed and broadcast it through the web.

FIGURE 5-10:
Ustream.tv lets you easily stream a live video of your presentation by plugging in your video camera to your computer and connecting with the service. Livestream, a similar service, allows you to easily toggle between live video and slides.

Once you've set up the live video feed, you'll get an URL you can then embed into your web page—then you're ready to stream.

If you can't offer a live stream because you don't have the equipment or bandwidth, consider using a web conferencing service to display a live feed of at least your voice and slides. Services such as Dimdim (www.dimdim.com) offer ways to integrate the meeting directly into web pages.

Embedding a backchannel tool

After adding a live video feed, consider adding a backchannel tool to the home page to foster conversation directly around the presentation.

One option is to add a custom chat tool that you create specifically for the meeting. This is probably the most elegant solution because some of the chat rooms include an interface where attendees can type directly into a text entry box and publish their backchannel posts there; they don't need to open up another browser. To reach a wider audience, you need to let people outside the event know exactly where to access the backchannel chat room, and you need to explain how they can use it.

> **tip ❯** As you learned in Chapter 2, there are a range of backchannel tools besides Twitter, each with its advantages and disadvantages. If you do choose to use a chat room or another tool for a backchannel, be sure to let people in your audience know so the backchannel is not split between your alternate tool and Twitter.

A good example of the advantage of integrating a live video stream and backchannel tool is the page created for the NECC 2009 conference (**Figure 5-11**). The top of the page features a live video feed of a presentation; the bottom of the page displays a chat room using the chat room feature provided by Ustream.tv.

Though the video and the chat room are hosted by Ustream.tv, they were placed here by pasting the Ustream.tv link code into the web page.

The placement of the video and the backchannel create a powerful synergy because the commentary is in the visual context of what's being said in the room.

Another option is to add a Twitter backchannel by using a third-party application or widget to pull a Twitter search feed to your page based on your event hashtag. As you previously learned, Twitter is a powerful way to bring a bigger audience into your presentations because the tweets go outward from the room to your audiences' Twitter followers around the world.

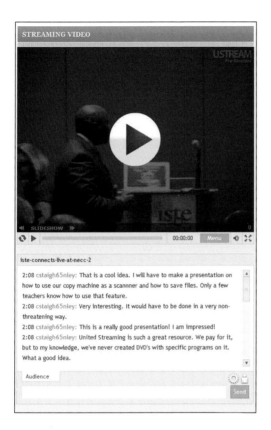

FIGURE 5-11:
This NECC 2009 conference page features a streaming video feed of live presentations next to a live chat room where people both inside the room and out participate in the backchannel. Embedding a backchannel tool next to the live video feed provides context for backchannel comments.

Preserving the life of the presentation well beyond the day

Your presentation home page relies on each hosting service making the materials available well after the presentation has come and gone. In case the providers have service difficulties, fail to archive the materials, or otherwise go out of business, be sure to archive a copy of the materials yourself:

- Copy and paste all of your wiki content into a word-processing or note-taking document.
- Copy and paste all of the backchannel comments into a document.
- Download a copy of your videos and store them locally.

With all of these key elements still in place, including an archived copy, your presentation home page can stay alive with ideas and with a community long after the applause has ended.

Facilitating a Backchannel in the Room

Now that you have set up an online home for your presentation, turn your attention to the physical room where you'll present your ideas.

Providing wireless Internet connectivity

Audiences these days expect to have wireless and phone access at meetings and events so they're able to connect to the Internet via laptops and smartphones. If there's no wireless access, the host leaves the impression the event is either behind the times or intentionally trying to stifle communications.

Work with your hosts to make sure they provide for more than enough wireless capacity to handle your audience's needs. This may be challenging when a host chooses a location without adequate access or uses basement-level meeting rooms where wireless and phone coverage are limited or nonexistent.

A couple of recent conferences did not allocate enough wireless capacity to handle the needs of the audience, which caused a backchannel blackout. If you have technical glitches, Twitter followers won't hesitate to quickly share the bad news with the world, making it all that much more important to get the tech side right.

> **tip ❯** Providing a wireless connection is as essential as providing water and clean restrooms. Audiences quickly become used to being connected, and if for some reason they lose Internet connection, they can get extremely upset. Make sure you have enough capacity to handle all the wireless activity you could possibly need, and then some.

Assigning a dedicated Twitter reporter

People who live-Twitter from your event provide a valuable stream of information that serves as a record of the event and a way to reach people who are not there.

The downside of live-Twittering is that it can be distracting if many people do it, and it can be redundant if people are reporting the same information.

Some event organizers seek out a volunteer to be a dedicated Twitter note-taker in turn for free admission to the event. If other audience members know there is a dedicated Twitter reporter they can trust, it saves them from having to do the job themselves.

Be selective with those you choose for this role: They should be journalists or excellent writers who have the skills to report accurately and quickly.

Considering whether to display the backchannel on stage

Some hosts will set up a screen onstage that has the live display of the backchannel chat onscreen to provide visual access for those who don't have the technical ability to join it or who simply choose not to. Or it may be an effort on the part of the hosts to welcome the backchannel.

Both are good intentions, but the negative impact of a projected backchannel during a live presentation often outweighs the positive impact it may bring.

Three Reasons To Not Display the Backchannel on Stage

When you display a backchannel on stage you run the risk of

1. Adding extraneous information to a live presentation, which hinders learning.
2. Splitting attention between the live speaker and the screen.
3. Encouraging people to add comments that call attention to themselves rather than the presenter.

There may be certain times when it's useful to display the backchannel, but otherwise don't show it on stage. Let those who wish to monitor the backchannel do so from laptops and smartphones.

As a presenter, you should use projected media to illustrate your ideas in an effort to keep your audience focused on the ideas. If a backchannel is displayed onscreen, the magnified image of the backchannel visually dominates the room and may distract your audience. In addition, backchannel posts are frequently off topic, not synchronized with what a speaker is saying, and full of otherwise extraneous information.

According to speaker Jared Spool:

> It's a bad idea to have Twitter on the screen during a live presentation. Twittering is an outbound experience, but putting Twitter on the screen makes it an inbound experience. The screen itself becomes the focus, rather than the person in the room.

Presentation coach Olivia Mitchell points out, however, that "there may be situations where it's appropriate to display the Twitterstream." For example:

- When you use polling tools that specifically integrate with Twitter (such as Poll Everywhere) to pull specific tweets.
- When you have a panel discussion and the panelists want to take questions via Twitter and display them to the room.
- When a presenter wants input via Twitter and wants it displayed to the audience.

In any case, as the presenter, you decide whether displaying Twitter on a screen on stage aids understanding of your message or distracts from it. If you arrive at an event and there is already a backchannel display on stage, make sure you can turn it off and on when you decide. In the worst-case scenario, you can always unplug the monitor.

Of course it's perfectly fine to display the backchannel between presentations or in the hallways (**Figure 5-12**). In those contexts, the screens are entertaining and they create an atmosphere of community because you see what's on the minds of your fellow attendees.

FIGURE 5-12:
Displaying a backchannel on a screen during breaks between sessions adds ambient visual interest.
(Courtesy of Daniel Dura)

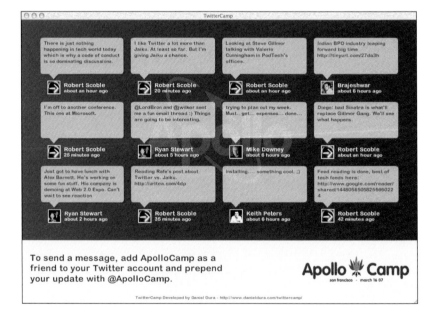

Working with the Host on the Fundamentals

After you've considered the big context for your ideas and built an online home for your presentation, you need to work on your presentation specifics. Be proactive with the meeting hosts and discuss with them how you can work together to get the fundamentals in place for an engaging backchannel experience.

Creating and promoting an event hashtag

As described in previous chapters, a hashtag is necessary for a Twitter backchannel to exist. Creating a hashtag is as simple as choosing a short combination of characters to designate your event and preceding it by a hashtag. To be sure you aren't using a hashtag that someone else is already using, do a quick search first for your proposed hashtag on http://search.twitter.com.

If you're having a single meeting, you'll only need a single hashtag, such as *#XYZ*. If you're at a larger event, differentiate individual meetings by assigning a hashtag for each one, which will make the backchannel easier to manage for each separate gathering. For example, create hashtag *#XYZmktg* for a marketing meeting, hashtag *#XYZstrat* for a strategy meeting, and *#XYZfin* for a finance meeting. Create hashtags using as few characters as possible so they don't use up too many of the 140-character limits that make up a tweet.

> **tip ❯** Many audience members bring digital cameras to events and post their photos on the photo-sharing website Flickr. To make the photos easy to find and share, encourage your audience members to use the same hashtag for participating in a Twitter backchannel and for adding identifying tags to photographs on Flickr.

Include the hashtags in all publicity and marketing materials from the outset; this tells your audience that you're welcoming the backchannel from the start. Another good place to promote your hashtag is where you welcome guests; include the hashtag on signs at the registration booth, on name tags, on the printed program, on carry totes, and so on.

Tweet about the event and your presentation

If you're a host, you'll want to send tweets from your account as described in Chapter 2. **Figure 5-13** shows sample tweets a host might send informing followers of the event.

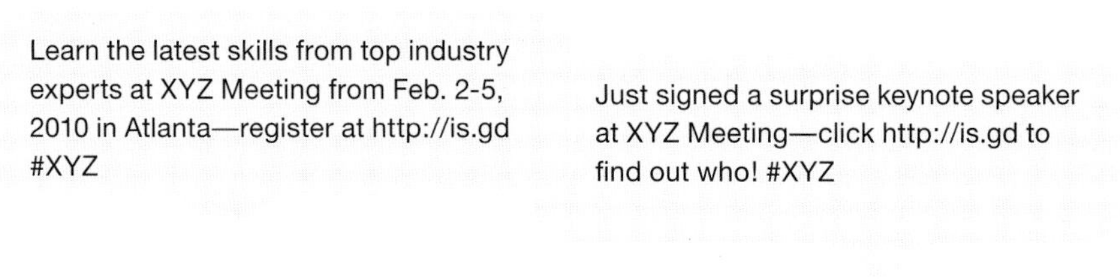

FIGURE 5-13:
If you're a host, describe your event and include your registration link and the event hashtag.

Learn the latest skills from top industry experts at XYZ Meeting from Feb. 2-5, 2010 in Atlanta—register at http://is.gd #XYZ

Just signed a surprise keynote speaker at XYZ Meeting—click http://is.gd to find out who! #XYZ

If you're a presenter, reach out to your blog readers, Twitter followers, email subscribers, or other online communities. Let them know about your upcoming event so they can either attend it themselves or spread the word to others.

Since your existing readers and followers are likely to be interested in your ideas, brainstorm with the host on ways to market your presentation to those who may attend in person. For example, if the host can offer and track discounts, you can promote this discount to your blog and Twitter followers by providing a link or code with this discount. **Figure 5-14** shows sample tweets you might send to your followers.

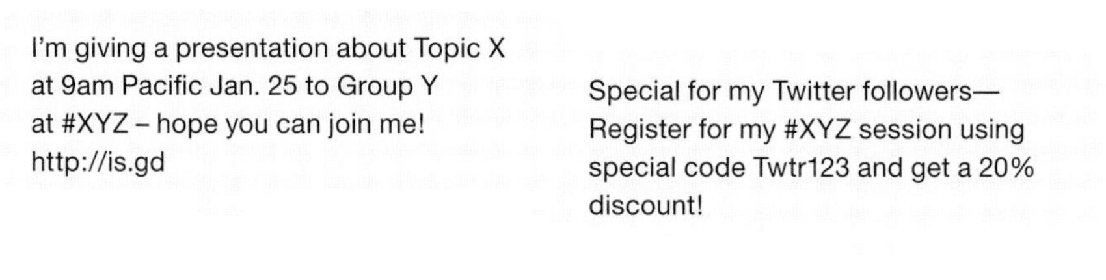

FIGURE 5-14:
If you're a presenter, let your followers know about your events and work with the host to offer discounts for your followers.

I'm giving a presentation about Topic X at 9am Pacific Jan. 25 to Group Y at #XYZ – hope you can join me! http://is.gd

Special for my Twitter followers— Register for my #XYZ session using special code Twtr123 and get a 20% discount!

It's also good practice to post the hashtag on your blog and Twitter before your presentation starts so those who can't attend in person are still able to attend the Twitter backchannel discussion.

Getting Ready To Get Your Content Ready

Preparing for the backchannel requires big shifts in thinking and shifts in creating platforms for your ideas and in logistics.

Once you're prepared for the changes that lie ahead in the new world of the backchannel, it's time to look at how you can make your ideas more digestible by making them Twitter-friendly.

[6]

Making Your Ideas Twitter-Friendly

To make your ideas easier for the
backchannel to understand and spread,
present your most important ideas
in Twitter-sized chunks

One of the reasons Twitter is so wildly popular is because of its constraints—the limit of 140 characters per tweet forces writers to cut out the fluff and get right to the point. It also forces writers to cut down large bodies of information into bite-sized chunks—or more specifically, Twitter-sized chunks.

This micro-format for information serves an important need for people today who are in the midst of an information explosion.

Becoming a Filter for Your Audiences

One of the biggest challenges facing any presenter today—whether you have a backchannel or not—is how to get your ideas across to an audience whose attention is distracted by so many different messages delivered in so many different forms.

More information, moving faster than ever

As a presenter, you have a great deal of information inside your mind, and within that context you have a subset of information that you want to convey to your audience through your presentation. Your audience already has information on their minds, and that information competes every moment with the information you would like them to pay attention to.

As earlier chapters described, the backchannel opens up many new channels of information—among people in the room, people outside the room, and people who wander outside of the room and then come back in. These new channels serve only to increase both the amount of information and the speed of information flowing during a presentation (**Figure 6-1**).

FIGURE 6-1:
These days people face increasingly large and fast-moving streams of information.

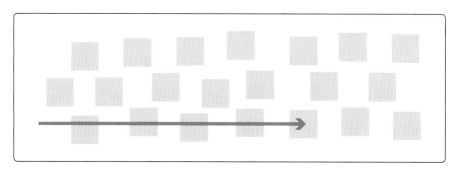

Though new information can be a good thing, there's a problem.

Running into the limits of the human mind

The reality of the human mind is that it is limited in its ability to process new information. Though we have potentially unlimited capacity to store information in long-term memory, and potentially unlimited capacity to scan the environment with sensory memory, we have severely limited capacity to pay attention to new information with working memory.

Memory scientist Nelson Cowan estimates that we can hold two to six independent ideas in our working memories, and we hold three to four on average.

Despite these limits, presenters still tend to assume that the more they present, the more information an audience will receive. That's simply not true—presenting more information than the mind can handle harms learning. And in a potentially distracting context like that presented by a backchannel, it becomes even more crucial that you choose the right amount of information to present to an audience.

In need of a filter—you!

With greater amount of inputs moving at a faster speed, there's an essential need for a filter—and that filter can be you. One of your roles as a presenter is to help make sense of things during your presentation. You have to do the editing, curating, and taste-making; you have to separate the informational wheat from the meaningless chaff in an effort to offer a tasty meal of insight, knowledge, and ideas.

Your goal then is to filter out the most relevant information to your audience (**Figure 6-2**).

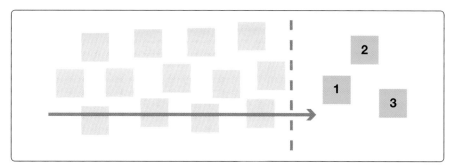

FIGURE 6-2:
Your challenge as a presenter is to filter out the most important information your audience needs to hear.

As you become a filter for your audience, you

- Reduce the volume of information delivered to your audience.
- Reduce the speed that the information is delivered to your audience.
- Allow only the most important information to reach your audience.

This helps both you and your audience to focus on and engage the right information during the time you have together.

Defining Your Most Important Points

The difficult task before you is to make fewer yet more important points and to present them in a way that your audience can absorb. Presentations are valuable today as opportunities for us to focus on a few important things together.

But a presentation can't focus on just anything. It has to focus on the right things—the things that the audience wants and needs to hear.

Viewing your presentation from the backchannel, not the podium

The next time you consider what you'll present from the podium, try starting with the view from the backchannel instead.

If you could step into the future today and read the Twitterstream feedback from your next presentation, ask yourself

- What do I want to read here?
- What factors could I use to determine if my presentation was successful?
- What ideas do I hope my audience re-tweets to others about my presentation?

Let's make this exercise practical by completing a worksheet to help you answer these questions.

Using the Four Tweets Worksheet

Turn to Appendix A, which provides the worksheet shown in **Figure 6-3**.

FIGURE 6-3:
The Four Tweets worksheet is based on a Twitter search results page. It provides room to write one summary tweet and three supporting tweets you would like to see your audience post.

The worksheet is built from a Twitter search results page and features space to write four results. The challenge is for you to draft the four most important ideas you would like your audience members to tweet to their followers.

To begin the challenge, think about who, exactly, will attend the presentation. If you already know the names of specific people who are representative of the larger audience or who are key decision makers, write their names here.

> ## Presentation Scenario: An Energy Company Executive
>
> As an example to illustrate the scenarios in this chapter, picture yourself as an executive at an energy company. You are preparing a presentation to give to your fellow executives to help them have a successful third quarter. You have a great deal of information you could possibly present within the 15 minutes you have to present. Your challenge is to narrow your material to only the most important information your audience needs to know.

Next, visualize what these audience members look like and then sketch pictures next to their names to show what they look like. Part of the power of a Twitter backchannel is that you see in the Twitterstream a photo of the person who wrote a comment, rather than just a name. When you sketch a picture of each audience member, you attach a comment to the face of a person, rather than leaving things abstract.

Now prepare to draft some preliminary tweets. Put yourself in the position of the authors of the posts while you keep in mind how they might actually compose tweets:

- They will be writing in first person, as they see you and your presentation through their eyes.
- They are writing to their audience of followers—people who trust what they have to say.
- They are limited to a maximum of 140 characters per post.
- If they include a link, they'll use an URL shortener to make it briefer.

Because you're writing your Twitter posts on a piece of paper, you won't be able to easily count your characters, so do a visual scan of the character count and aim to keep the lines as brief as possible.

The Rule of Four Tweets

Now, your challenge as you complete the rest of this chapter is to apply the Rule of Four Tweets. The rule states that no matter what your topic, you should distill all of the information you'd like to present to only

- A single summary tweet that describes the essence of your entire presentation in 140 characters or less.
- Three supporting tweets that explain your summary tweet in further detail.

Together these tweets should be the most important things you'd like your audience to tell others they learned from your presentation.

The Full Ten Tweets Challenge

Although this chapter focuses only on distilling your presentation to four tweets, the Ten Tweets worksheet in Appendix B provides ten tweets for you to more fully prepare for your presentation:

- In tweets one through four, write the four tweets, as described in this chapter.
- In tweets five and six, write the links to the two most useful resources from your presentation that you'd like your audience to pass on to other people.
- In tweets seven and eight, sketch the two slides you'd like your audience to photograph.
- In tweets nine and ten, write two tweets that describe how you would like your audience to describe your delivery.

The value of the four tweets is tremendous because in these brief 140-character posts you'll get to the point of your presentation and make your ideas easy to re-tweet.

Breaking Up Your Ideas into Twitter-sized Chunks

Your four tweets will be brief, and writing them will be hard work, but it will be well worth the effort when you fill in the Twitter blanks (**Figure 6-4**). On the surface, they are useful takeaways for your audience; beneath the surface, writing the four tweets offers a host of clarifying benefits.

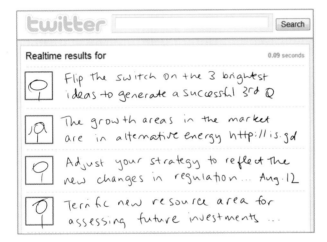

FIGURE 6-4:
Writing your four tweets helps you distill your ideas so you know what to emphasize during your presentation.

Defining the most important things you want your audience to learn

Experienced speakers agree that an effective presentation is not centered on the presenter but rather on the audience and how you help them learn new ideas and apply them to their lives. Social media expert Chris Brogan puts it this way:

Presentations are a way to move information from my head into your actions. If I do it right, I give my ideas "handles," so that you can run with what I've started and make it your own.

In order to put handles on your own ideas, you have to know exactly what you want your audiences to learn so that you can present it appropriately.

According to educational psychologist Richard E. Mayer, when you give a multimedia presentation to an audience, there are three possible outcomes:

- **No learning:** In spite of the time you spent with your audience, no measurable learning occurred.
- **Fragmented learning:** Bits and pieces of information made it through, but you're not sure exactly which pieces they were.
- **Meaningful learning:** What you intended your audience to remember and apply actually happened in a measurable way.

If you're not clear about the most important tweets you want your audience to post, the likely outcome of your approach will be fragmented learning—because you yourself are unsure about the relative importance of the information in your presentation. If you're not clear about what's most important, your audience won't be clear either.

But when you write the four tweets, you crystallize in your own mind what you want your audiences to learn and thereby improve the chances they'll actually learn it.

Going through the learning process from your audience's perspective

One of the most difficult processes you have to go through as a presenter is to take information and somehow structure it so that it's as easy as possible for your audience to digest. The problem is that you have spent extensive time immersed in the knowledge, but your audience has not. And once you know information, it's difficult to step back and explain it to someone who does not have that knowledge.

When you write the four tweets, you look at your information through new eyes—the eyes of your audience.

Think about what has to happen in order for your audience members to write the four tweets on their laptops or smart phones then click the button to publish them in the Twitterstream.

First of all, you're likely to be presenting to strangers who are meeting you for the first time, and they are unlikely to write what you tell them to write—not before they experience your live presentation and get a sense of whether they like and trust you. Next, they'll listen to your ideas. If they find anything useful, and they think their Twitter followers will find it useful, they're likely to write about it on Twitter.

So how do you get from *here* (where you're probably not sure what your most important ideas are) to *there* (where your audience is interested enough in your ideas that they want to share them with their friends and colleagues)?

A little audience reverse engineering is in order. Start from the desired outcome and work your way back to the current situation. As you go through the steps of looking at the learning process from your audience's perspective, you'll improve their odds of learning the new material.

Tapping into the power of brevity

Writing a brief Twitter post about enjoying breakfast or the latest movie is easy; but it's another story altogether to take some rich and meaningful piece of information and distill it down to 140 characters or less.

That's the challenge that people in the backchannel accept every time they live-Twitter from an event: how to convey the gist of what someone is saying while still retaining its meaning. When Twitter writers are good, their posts are pithy slices of meaning served up from a good presentation.

The benefits of brevity are even more powerful on the presentation side, when you can boil down the essence of your message to a Twitter post or four. When you get to the point, you eliminate the extraneous information that creates clutter—clutter that stands in the way of understanding and learning new information.

Creating a way to measure your results

When you aim for your audience to post the most important ideas you want to convey, you create a concrete way to determine your effectiveness, since it will be the actions of your audiences that determine success.

After the presentation, your event's Twitterstream will reveal exactly how good a job you did. You may find your audiences posted the four tweets exactly as you hoped. Or you may find that there were other tweets that were even better than what you had anticipated. In that case, you may want to take those better tweets and incorporate them into your material for future presentations.

Either way, you'll have a measurable way to determine how well you did in your presentation and how you can improve your message next time.

Putting Your Four Tweets in the Context of a Story

One of the most powerful tools you can use to organize your ideas is a classic story structure. Though normally applied to fictional stories, the story structure is perfectly appropriate for your nonfiction story as well.

The set up is as simple as three elements (**Figure 6-5**):

- What challenge does the main character (your audience) face at Point A?

- Where do they want to be at Point B?

- How they get from Point A to Point B? The gap between points A and B creates the dramatic tension that drives any story forward. When you close the gap between points A and B, you create your story line.

FIGURE 6-5:
A classic structure includes a main character who faces a challenge at Point A and would like to get to Point B—the story line is how they get there.

For example, as the executive of an energy company a challenge your fellow executives face at Point A is that they are so overwhelmed by choices that they face the real possibility that their strategy will unravel. In the face of that challenge, where they want to be at Point B is to know which choices to make to pull the situation back together. How do they get from Point A (a state of overwhelm) to Point B (confidence to make the right decisions)? They follow your story line, which is: "Pull together three strategy threads to tie up a successful third quarter."

For nonfiction story structures, include these elements at the start of every presentation to connect with your audiences emotionally, make the material relevant, and lay out the narrative path.

> **tip >** For step-by-step instructions on how to create a presentation using a story structure, see my book *Beyond Bullet Points* (Microsoft Press, 2007).

As you fashion your story structure at the start, your summary tweet should describe how your audience can get from Point A to Point B, and your supporting tweets should explain your summary (**Figure 6-6**).

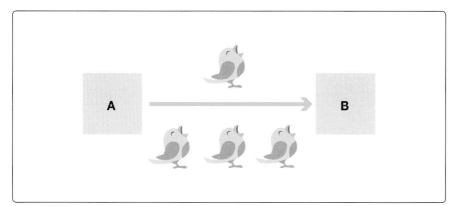

FIGURE 6-6:
Your four tweets should be the way your audience gets from the challenge they face at Point A to where they want to be at Point B.

In the energy company example, your summary tweet is "Flip the switch on the three brightest ideas to generate a successful third quarter http://is.gd" and your three supporting tweets would explain how your audience would accomplish that:

- The growth areas in the market are in alternative energy—for detailed trends see http://is.gd

- Adjust your strategy to reflect the new changes in regulation that go into effect Aug. 12—see http://is.gd

- Terrific new resource area for assessing future investments—just gave it a try at http://is.gd and loved it!

In effect, your four tweets become the solution to the problem your audience faces—how to get from Point A to Point B. This classic problem-solution structure is a rock-solid foundation for your presentation and a way to provide a narrative that ties your tweets together.

When you have a story structure in mind, you can either present it verbally or create slides that illustrate your points, which we'll cover shortly.

Linking your tweets with a metaphor

If you tie together your four tweets with a metaphor, you improve the chances your audience will remember your key points and pass them on.

For example, the energy presentation uses the metaphor of a power grid to "flip the switch" on the three brightest ideas. You could also set up your three supporting tweets as steps to get somewhere, three clues to solve a mystery, or three ingredients to a recipe. Metaphors like these are a form of cognitive shorthand—people are already familiar with their basic structures, and by applying this familiarity to your new ideas, you help people to understand them better.

> **tip >** For an excellent resource on finding metaphors for your presentations (and tweets), see Anne Miller's book *Metaphorically Selling* (Chiron Associates, 2004).

When you have a story structure in place, you're ready to start distilling your ideas into your four tweets.

Beginning the Process of Distilling Your Ideas

Deciding on the top four tweets you want your audience to write is easier said than done. You could say thousands of things during your next presentation, yet you need to choose the most important things out of all of those possible choices.

Writing the four tweets involves some of the hardest work you'll do, because to get there, you have to go through a rigorous critical thinking process.

Jay Cuthrell describes this work in a blog post as follows:

> *More than anything, I think the process is one of distilling a given topic into a potent residual memory. Just like a stiff drink, you want them to remember it.*

Brainstorming and mind mapping your ideas

The start of any presentation begins with your ideas, which may not have firm shape yet as you explore the range of possibilities before you. A range of techniques and tools can help you with that process, including

- Software-based techniques, such as mind mapping, that help you easily and quickly group ideas and explore synergies.
- Tools such as whiteboards, sticky notes, and sketchpads that help you put abstract ideas onto paper (**Figure 6-7**).

FIGURE 6-7:
Begin brainstorming your ideas to create the raw material that you'll distill into your four tweets.

It doesn't matter what process you choose; the right one is the one that generates the ideas that you need to start assembling the body of your presentation.

Grouping, clustering, narrowing, editing

The next step is to start applying your critical-thinking skills to figure out what it all means. Here you might group ideas, narrow down possibilities, and look for patterns. As you start seeing relationships among ideas, some common themes will likely start to emerge, forming the foundation of what might be useful to your audience.

As you cut down the volume of ideas, edit your ideas ruthlessly to get to the points you want to make. Author Kathy Sierra writes in her blog,

> It's far more important that (people) nail the key things than be exposed to everything. Be brutal, be brave, be relentless in what you leave out. Knowing what NOT to include is more important...than knowing what TO include.

Distilling is not cutting down your ideas so much that your audience won't understand what you're saying, nor is it dumbing down your ideas to the lowest common denominator. Rather, when you distill your ideas you make them simpler to understand, but you're not losing the integrity of your critical thinking that backs them up.

Distilling should be a process of finding the essence of your ideas in the briefest form possible, which you'll then articulate in the form of a few Twitter posts.

Hierarchy is dead; long live hierarchy

The most effective tool you can use to distill your ideas to four tweets is *hierarchy*.

When most people think of hierarchy, they think of an organizational chart like the one shown in **Figure 6-8** that illustrates the relationships among people in a social group. Following the standard convention of organizational charts, the person represented by the top box is in charge of the three people represented by the three bottom boxes.

FIGURE 6-8:
A hierarchy is commonly used to describe social relationships as in an organizational chart.

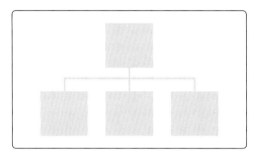

Hierarchical organizational charts may still be common, but they no longer hold favor among those who see social systems today as less structured and more flexible than rigid command and control views of times past.

In many ways, social media tools such as blogs, YouTube, and Twitter have flattened social hierarchies at astonishing speed. Before social media, anyone with ideas to publish appealed to newspaper editors to expose the idea to the public; now anybody with a computer and a blog can do it. In the past, anyone who had an idea for a video appealed to video companies to produce and distribute them; now anybody with a video camera and a YouTube account can do it.

Yet it's ironic that at the same time social media is flattening social hierarchies, it has increased the need for another kind of hierarchy: *information hierarchy*. Though we may be able to escape the bounds of social hierarchy, we are not yet able to escape the bounds of cognitive hierarchy—the reality that we have to figure out what's most important in order to understand it.

Scientists describe human memory as working in a hierarchical fashion. Since we can't possibly access all the information in our minds at one time, we access the top-level information we need and then deeper levels of detail when we need it.

So we still do need hierarchy in presentations—just not in the social sense. We need it to help organize information in ways that help us immediately see the most important information before us.

When you use a hierarchy to organize information, you put your most important information at the top of the hierarchy and your supporting information below it (**Figure 6-9**).

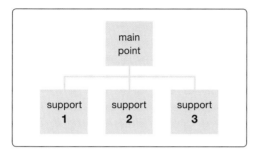

FIGURE 6-9:
When you create an information hierarchy, you put the most important information at the top—the main point you are making—and then the supporting ideas beneath it.

Then when you present information, you move from the top down—you make your main point, and then communicate the support for that main point. You don't present the supporting ideas first; there's no context for the details. Rather you present the main point first to provide direction and then proceed through the detail.

For example, in the energy presentation, you state "Pull together three strategy threads" (your main point in the form of a summary tweet) before you go into the detail of explaining what those strategy threads actually are (your explanation in the form of your three supporting tweets).

This is a powerful way to avoid information overload because you are always elevating the main point and presenting that main point first, cutting through the information clutter and clearing a pathway for the details to come.

When you integrate this hierarchical structure with the story structure described earlier, your main point is the story arc that takes your audience from Point A to Point B; your supporting points back up your main point (**Figure 6-10** on the next page).

> **tip ❯** If you're familiar with the presentation approach in my book *Beyond Bullet Points*, you'll find this blend of hierarchy and story familiar in the BBP Story Template. With BBP, however, the main point is called the *Call to Action* slide and the supporting points are called the *Key Point* slides.

FIGURE 6-10:
Blending both
hierarchical and
story structures
brings together both
logic and emotion.

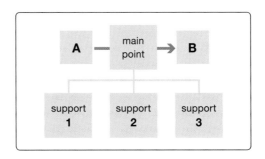

When you use a hierarchical structure, you appeal to logic because you make a point and back it up with support. When you use a story structure, you appeal to emotion because you create an unresolved state of emotional tension between where your audience is and where they want to be. And when you bring together both hierarchical and story structures, you create a powerful blended appeal to both emotion and reason.

Floating a presentation iceberg in an information sea

In developing a simple hierarchical structure, you could outline its shape to reveal a pyramid (**Figure 6-11**). The tip is where you put information that is more important; the base is where you put supporting information.

FIGURE 6-11:
A pyramid defines
the shape of a
hierarchy.

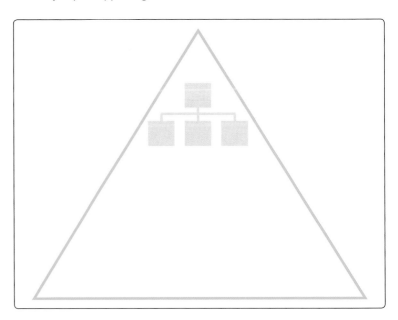

In terms of your presentation, look at the pyramid as an opportunity to define the boundaries of all of the information you could possibly relate during a presentation.

> **tip ❯** For a powerful method of applying hierarchy to your ideas, see Barbara Minto's book entitled *The Minto Pyramid Principle: Logic in Writing, Thinking and Problem Solving* (Minto Books International, 2007).

One of the important things you learned in Chapter 5 was how to use your presentation home page as a repository for the detailed information you don't have time to present. When you do that, you create a boundary between what you will present during the live presentation (offline) and what you will link to on the web (online).

To reflect the boundary between your offline information and your online information, submerge your pyramid in water, leaving one portion sitting above the waterline and one below it (**Figure 6-12**).

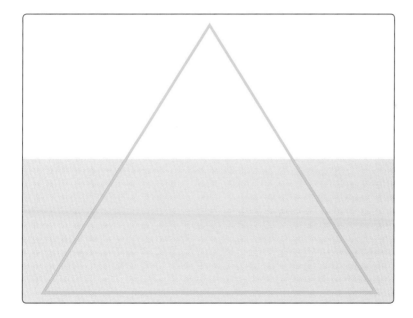

FIGURE 6-12: Submerging the pyramid shape in water creates a dividing line.

What you've created is a presentation iceberg floating in the information sea. And like a real iceberg, there's much more to it than meets the eye.

Of all the information in the sea, you've bounded what's possible to present within the shape of the iceberg. The most important information is that which is visible above the water. The rest of the information is made available on the presentation home page (**Figure 6-13** on the next page).

FIGURE 6-13:
Above the line is what you present during a live presentation. Below the line are all the resources you post on the presentation home page

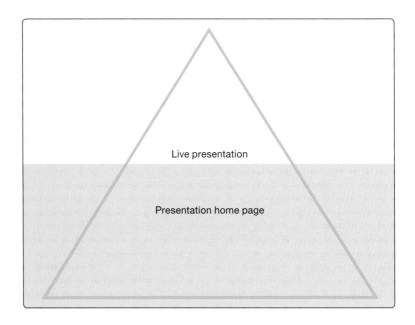

Now when you look at your presentation iceberg, your most important information (in the form of your summary tweet) sits at the tip, followed by your three supporting tweets (**Figure 6-14**), clearly articulating the essence of your message.

FIGURE 6-14:
The four tweets should distill everything you have to present both in the live presentation and on the presentation home page.

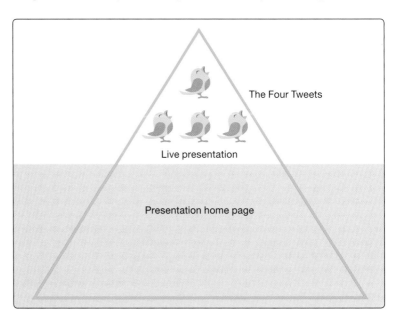

With this approach in place, your four tweets aren't random; they are intentional and meaningful pieces of information that fit within a larger framework. The information you choose for your in-person presentation also is not random; it's the most important information that explains your four tweets. And the information you refer and link to on your presentation home page is not random; it is what gives your ideas the intellectual foundation and integrity to stand on.

Unlocking the power of the pyramid

Finally, when you include links to your presentation home page in your four tweets, you create a dynamism that unlocks the full power of your presentation (**Figure 6-15** on the next page).

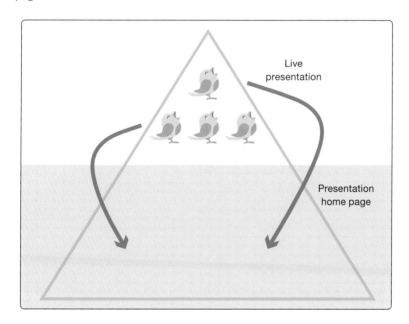

Live
presentation

Presentation
home page

FIGURE 6-15:
Link your four tweets to a specific location where your audiences—and their audiences— can find more information on your topic.

Now these tiny four tweets at the top are chock-full of meaning, linking back to the online information people can explore at their leisure.

In the energy presentation example, each tweet features a link (using an URL short-ener) that points readers back to resources located on the presentation home page.

Expressing a singular hierarchy through multiple mediums

When you know your most important ideas in the form of your four tweets, you can reinforce the importance of the ideas through

- Emphasis with voice and facial expression.
- Gestures and body movement.
- Pauses for effect.
- Audience involvement.
- Video and sound.

The combined effect should be a reinforcement of your ideas in multiple ways up and down the information hierarchy.

Writing Your Four Tweets on Four Slides

Before you complete your Four Tweets Worksheet, you need to know the characteristics of good backchannel tweets:

- **They are a complete sentence written in active voice, present tense, and using conversational tone.** When you make a complete thought in the form of a sentence, people will understand the message faster and easier.

- **They're actually less than 140 characters.** These posts need to be shorter than usual because when a post is re-tweeted, a few extra characters are added to the post. If your post is shorter to begin with, it's not only easier for your audience to re-tweet, it reduces the risk someone will delete essential information.

- **They're useful.** Lastly, your tweets will be even more likely to be re-tweeted if you offer a link to something others might find useful. In the energy presentation example, each tweet offered a link to further information available on the presentation home page.

    tip ❯ As you're drafting your four tweets, use a Twitter application or a free online tool (such as the Cut & Paste Character Count tool from www.javascriptkit.com) to count the number of characters you have in your draft tweets.

If you're looking for more examples of how to write your four tweets, visit the Twitter home pages of people you follow who are good at getting their points across in short form. If you don't already follow people on Twitter, see the section entitled "Following other people" in Chapter 2 and choose people to follow whose writing style you like. Or scan newspapers, magazines, and websites to see what good copywriters and headline writers do to grab attention and get to the point as efficiently as possible.

When you've written your four tweets (**Figure 6-16**), you've achieved something significant. You've distilled your ideas to their essence, articulated them in a way that makes it easier for your audience to learn, and you've made them as easy possible to be passed on to others.

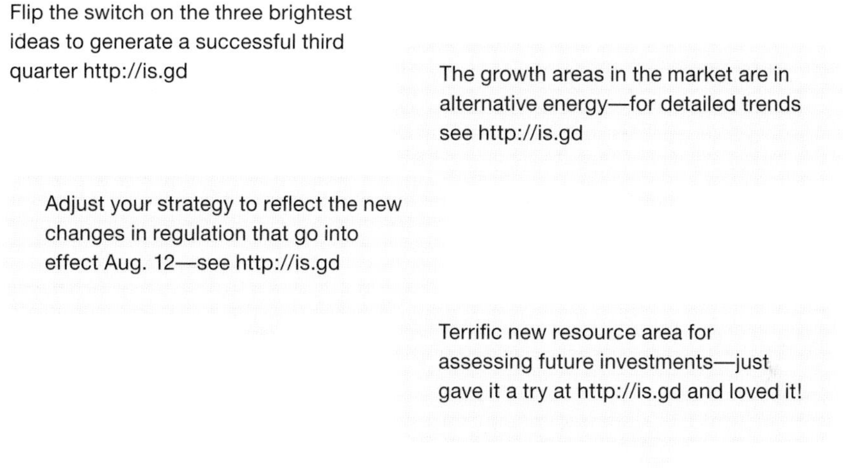

Flip the switch on the three brightest ideas to generate a successful third quarter http://is.gd

The growth areas in the market are in alternative energy—for detailed trends see http://is.gd

Adjust your strategy to reflect the new changes in regulation that go into effect Aug. 12—see http://is.gd

Terrific new resource area for assessing future investments—just gave it a try at http://is.gd and loved it!

FIGURE 6-16: Congratulations! You've completed the hard work of determining the most important ideas you'd like your audience to pass on to their own followers.

Now that you've got your essential four tweets, what's next?

To PowerPoint or not to PowerPoint— that is the question

Although we haven't used any presentation software yet, now that you've got in mind the main ideas you want to communicate, it's a good time to consider how you can bring them to visual life.

Presentation software is a tool that can be used in any number of ways, and audiences don't like to sit through a series of slides showing only bulleted points. Communications expert Jen McClure says she sees less use of PowerPoint these days, and that some speakers find the software irrelevant. Of the eight recent keynotes she observed, less than half the presenters used PowerPoint—and they used it mostly for screen shots, video, pictures, and graphs. They showed almost no text at all.

Researchers have discovered that we learn better from the combination of words and pictures than we do from just words alone. There are ways to use presentation software to tap into the value of combining words and pictures.

Whatever presentation tool you use (PowerPoint, Keynote, SlideRocket, or others), try building a visual story that you create from the most important information you have to convey—your four tweets.

Creating one slide for each tweet

To begin creating a few basic slides, open your presentation software program and create four slides with a title-only layout (**Figure 6-17**).

FIGURE 6-17:
Create four blank slides in your presentation software program with a title-only layout.

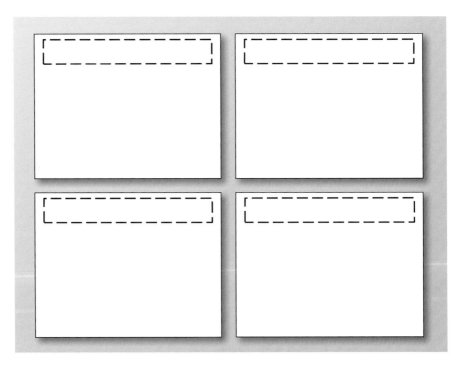

Tapping into the power of a headline

Just as you worked hard to create a hierarchy from all of your ideas, you also need to create an information hierarchy with your visuals to help your audience learn more effectively.

At the top of a slide, it's common to use a word or two to create a category heading (such as *Objectives* or *Lessons Learned*). These words are usually too brief to be of much meaning by themselves, so they push your audience's eyes to the rest of the slide, which contains the information they need to know to help make more sense of the headings.

A more effective approach is to use a complete sentence headline at the top of your slide. Research by Michael Alley reveals that we learn better when we read complete sentences as headlines rather than sentence fragments.

So where do you go to get your headlines? You already have them, in the form of your four tweets.

Writing headlines for your slides

Insert your cursor into the title area of your first slide and type the first of your four tweets, and then repeat this step for the next three slides to complete the set of four slides (**Figure 6-18**).

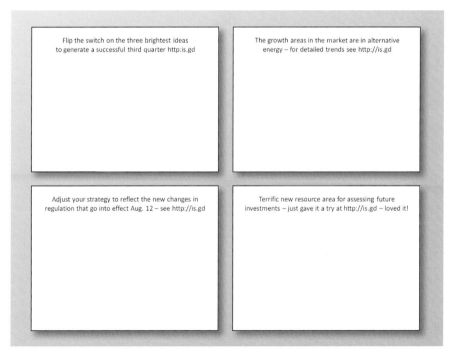

FIGURE 6-18:
Write your tweets directly into the title area of title-only slides in your presentation software program.

You may need to do a bit of editing to turn the four tweets into slide headlines. On the Four Tweets worksheet, you wrote your tweets from the point of view of your audience members as if they were tweeting them. But when you write a slide headline, you have to write it from your point of view as if you are saying the words, because you are the one doing the talking as you display the slides.

The first three tweets in this example work as slide headlines if you use them directly as you wrote them. The fourth tweet—*Terrific new resource area for assessing future investments—just gave it a try at http://is.gd and loved it!*—would not sound quite right as a slide headline because it includes the type of opinions (*terrific* and *loved it!*) that you hope your audience adds when they re-tweet it. Also, it's not a complete sentence.

To convert it to a headline, edit this last tweet to make it sound like it's coming from your voice and write it in the form of a complete sentence: *Give our new resource area a try to help you assess future investments.*

It's more effective to illustrate your points by adding a graphic, but if you're a slide minimalist or don't have time to find graphics, you can choose not to include graphics. You can improve their appearance a bit by adding a background color, choosing a contrasting font color for the text, enlarging the font size, and centering the titles. Since your summary tweet becomes the summary slide for your presentation, apply a different color background from the other three slides to make it stand out (**Figure 6-19**).

FIGURE 6-19:
To create a minimalist version of a presentation, enlarge the font size, change the background and font colors, and center the title on the page.

If that's as much as you want to do, you're finished with your presentation because you have your most important ideas on three slides. Just project each slide on the screen as you cover each point.

Adding graphics to your slides

If you'd like to tap into the power of visuals to make your point, add a graphic to each slide that illustrates the point you're making. **Figure 6-20** shows how you can use inexpensive photographs from iStockphoto.com to illustrate the headlines.

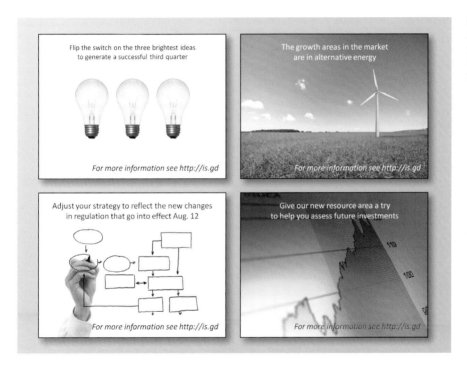

FIGURE 6-20:
Add stock photos to your three slides to illustrate the points you're making.

Now your audience can clearly understand your slide from top to bottom:

- A headline summarizes the point you're making.
- A graphic illustrates the headline.
- A link provides a place to additional information.
- And, of course, your voice and expressions provide detailed explanation and context.

> **tip ❯** The topic of adding graphics to your slides is worthy of a book unto itself. Fortunately, there are several good books out there if you're interested in learning more about presentation design, including Garr Reynolds' *Presentation Zen* (New Riders, 2008) and Nancy Duarte's *Slideology* (O'Reilly, 2008).

If you had only these four slides in your presentation, you would certainly reinforce your most important ideas and push them out to the world in the form of at least four tweets people find useful.

But audiences crave visual variety, and they want to hear more of your story, so now you'll learn how to unlock more presentation power from your four tweets.

Building Sections Around Your Tweets

Now that you have your most important ideas in mind, you need to craft the rest of your presentation within whatever timeframe you're working within—5 minutes, 15 minutes, 60 minutes, several hours (for a workshop), or even several days (for a seminar). A few techniques can help you present your tweets in as meaningful a context as possible.

Anchoring your tweets in three sections of a storyboard

Presenting to a backchannel demands a different way of structuring your information so that it's broken into digestible chunks, which is exactly what you did when you wrote your supporting tweets to explain your summary tweet. Since these three supporting tweets are the most important ideas you have to communicate, they naturally fit as introductions to each of the sections of your presentation that follow each supporting tweet.

To begin building your three sections, choose the slide sorter view of your presentation software, a feature that allows you to create and follow a story visually from one slide to the next. Insert three blank slides after each of your three supporting tweets (**Figure 6-21**). Using three slides is a good rule of thumb so you don't spend too much time on any single section.

FIGURE 6-21:
In slide sorter view, insert three blank slides after each of your supporting tweets to begin creating a storyboard that explains your ideas in more detail.

As you build the story structure described previously in this chapter and then add your tweets and additional slides, you're starting to see the storyboard emerge in slide sorter view.

Then as you explain each of your supporting tweets with three additional slides, you're creating three distinct sections of your presentation. By having three sections, you'll create natural places to pause for the Twitter breaks that you'll learn about in Chapter 7.

As you build a presentation this way, you're breaking up your bigger ideas into digestible chunks, and you're providing built-in pacing, variety, and a brain-friendly structure for your information.

Preparing Your Slides for Camera Phones and Handheld Video Cameras

Besides bringing laptops and Twitter into meeting rooms, your audience also brings camera phones, voice recorders, and video cameras to presentations. Even if you're not keen on the idea of being recorded, the reality these days is that there is little you can do to stop it.

Rather than fight the trend—unless you have truly sensitive or proprietary information you don't want broadcasted—consider those recording you as providing you with just one more way you can push your information to the world. In reality, it's a compliment when people go to the trouble of recording you, so do what you can to make their jobs easier.

Improving the accuracy of your ideas heading outside the room

These days it's not uncommon for audience members to take a pictures of slides to share on Twitter. One of the popular ways to share is by using TwitPic, which provides a link to the photo via Twitter. You can use TwitPic on your phone, through a Twitter client, or through the TwitPic website.

Help your audience get good TwitPics so that you can extend your ideas out to a much wider audience in a visual form. A TwitPic-friendly slide includes the characteristics of the slides you created earlier:

- A legible and meaningful headline.
- A clear and simple graphic.
- A link to find additional information.

Test your slides for photo-friendliness using your own digital camera to take a snapshot to see how they look on the small screen (**Figure 6-22**).

FIGURE 6-22:
When your slides have clear headlines, simple graphics, and links to additional information, they become photo-friendly ways to extend your message clearly and accurately.

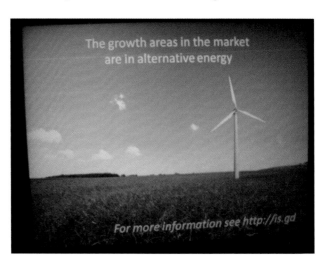

Considering video

Now that your ideas are Twitter-friendly and your slides are TwitPic-friendly, make sure your entire presentation is also friendly to live video streaming services such as Ustream.tv or Livestream (described in Chapter 5). When you set up the room, test the lighting through a video camera to make sure you are visible, and set up the best audio arrangement you can (this might mean using a separate microphone instead of the one built into the camera).

Getting Ready To Start the Conversation

When you've made your ideas more digestible and spreadable in the form of your four tweets, you're ready to engage and involve your audience. You'll learn this next in Chapter 7.

[7]

Joining the Backchannel in Conversation

Start a conversation with
the backchannel
before, during, and after
your presentation

n Chapter 3, you learned how the backchannel introduces completely new dynamics to face-to-face presentations.

Before the backchannel became available, a presentation and a conversation were two distinct activities. During a formal presentation, you (as presenter) were the only one talking; the audience did the listening. During an informal conversation, multiple people did the talking and the listening in turn.

By connecting people both inside and outside the room, the backchannel creates the potential for a *network conversation*—a hybrid of presentation and conversation. When there is a backchannel, a presenter still talks to an audience, but audience members inside and outside the room also talk to one another—as well as back to the presenter (**Figure 7-1**).

FIGURE 7-1:
The backchannel opens up new conversations among everyone involved in a presentation.

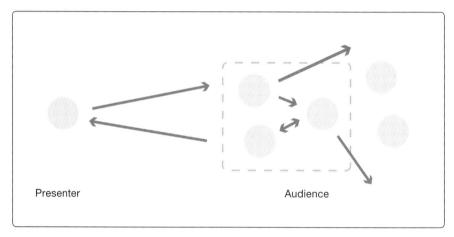

Presenter   Audience

This significant change in the room demands, in turn, an equally significant change in the evolution of our thinking about presentations.

Creating a Hybrid of Presentation and Conversation

Presentations and conversations have always offered benefits appropriate to the context in which they are used; it's just that now in the backchannel, these once-separate activities are happening at the same time. And when presenters and audiences talk at the same time, the situation is ripe for misunderstanding and conflict. As a result, there's a need to figure out a way to integrate presentations and conversations so they work well together.

A presentation offers structure and focus

A meeting normally involves primarily presentation or primarily conversation, and each has its pros and cons.

A presentation is a set of prepared remarks that presenters deliver to audiences. Though audiences might give verbal and visual cues that indicate they are listening, a presentation is essentially a one-way mode of communicating (except for any Q&A that might happen at the end).

A big benefit of a presentation is that it offers a structure and focus for a presentation experience so that you and your audience do not get lost or end up going in circles. You and your audience obviously want to get somewhere, and a presentation structure is the roadmap that will get you there.

But if a meeting is mostly a presentation with a bit of Q&A at the end (**Figure 7-2**), it's pretty much a lecture—and many backchannel audiences consider a one-way lecture as old as yesterday's bullet points.

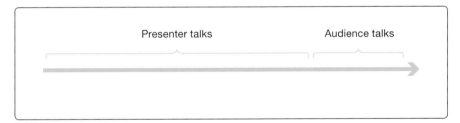

Presenter talks   Audience talks

FIGURE 7-2:
A meeting that is mostly presentation has the presenter doing most of the talking.

These days, backchannel audiences want both information and participation; they want more involvement, less one-way lecture.

A conversation offers involvement and spontaneity

A conversation is a dialogue between two or more people and offers a range of benefits that a presentation does not. In the course of dialogue, interesting and unscripted things can happen spontaneously.

A conversation implies that people are not passively receiving information and simply digesting it whole. Instead, they are actively listening, processing the information, and then engaging it when they reply.

But if a meeting is all conversation (**Figure 7-3**), the group might quickly meander—losing focus.

FIGURE 7-3:
A meeting that is mostly conversation has the audience doing the talking.

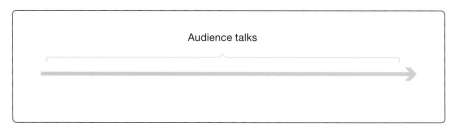

The often-meandering nature of conversation is perfectly fine in many contexts, but it's not suitable for the constraints created by the limited time and attention of audiences today.

A hybrid offers the best of both worlds

To manage the new network conversation of the backchannel, we need to bring together the best of presentations (structure and focus) with the best of conversations (spontaneity and involvement).

A conversational presentation is a hybrid that still offers the shape of a presentation structure but creates more space for conversation.

Instead of speaking all at once, presenters break up the presentation into sections. After each section, the presenters leave time for audiences to get involved in the action before proceeding to the next point (**Figure 7-4**).

FIGURE 7-4:
A hybrid presentation-conversation offers audiences a framework with more frequent breaks.

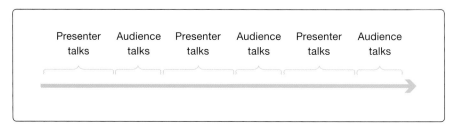

This provides more opportunities for conversation throughout the same timeframe, breaking a single one-way dynamic into more two-way interactions.

From a presenter's perspective, the heart of your conversation is the set of ideas you identified in Chapter 6, which you use to lay out the parameters of your presentation.

You know what you want to cover and, at the very least, you have a basic structure in place.

From an audience's perspective, they get a better opportunity to be involved with the presentation, making their contributions by voice or backchannel or through participating in exercises.

Giving your audience a structure and inviting them to fill in the blanks

By using this conversational presentation approach, you and your audience can have your presentation cake and eat it, too, because presentations and conversations no longer are separate activities.

As a presenter, the difference is that rather than delivering your audience a finished cake and asking them how it tasted, you give them a great recipe, the ingredients, and you ask them to make the cake with you.

By drawing out the broad outlines and letting the audience fill in the detail, you create a dynamic in which participants co-create the story that everyone then gets an opportunity to tell.

Adjusting to a More Conversational Presentation

Managing a conversational presentation involves a range of techniques you need to use to increase audience participation and prompt them to talk about your ideas before, during, and after your presentation.

These techniques call on you to develop ever more creative ways to help your audience learn new information and then apply it to the specific situations in their lives.

Making more time for involvement

As always, a presentation is defined by constraints. You're constrained by time. Your audience is constrained by the human mind's ability to learn new information.

You'd like to give your audience a chance to participate, but participation takes time—and where will you get the extra time when time is in such short supply these days? The answer is to cover less material and *make* more time for those things that are most important.

In Chapter 6, you learned how to determine what is most important by creating a hierarchy out of your ideas. Spend the most time on what is most important at the top of the hierarchy, then if needed send your audiences online to get any further details they might like to have. When you spend more time on more important information, you give the information more of a chance to sink in.

Making more room for involvement

As you move toward more involvement, your presentation starts to look more like a working session than a lecture.

The shift in format demands that your room be configured differently. For example, you might need to use round tables instead of rows of chairs and you might need to use whiteboards or flip charts in addition to projectors and screens.

Be sure to leave plenty of room for people to move around if you give your audience exercises to complete.

Learning to be a facilitator

By providing the framework for more involvement, speakers are still presenters but now they take on the additional role of guiding and facilitating the discussion—helping the audience find their own way and helping them learn by doing.

This involves listening, prompting, and summarizing what's happening as it's happening.

Helping everyone learn from one another

By loosening up your presentation structure, you'll certainly learn more from your audiences because they'll have an opportunity to say more. But you also create the conditions for your audiences to tap in to an underutilized resource in the room— each other. When you create opportunities for your audience members to engage one another, you allow them to discover new knowledge and relationships that would otherwise be locked away in the silent rows of a lecture hall.

What you do to adjust to a conversational structure doesn't have to be complicated. Doing just a few of the simple things covered in the following section makes a big impact and helps you reap the rewards the backchannel has to offer you and your audiences.

Starting the Backchannel Conversation Early

So how do you get the conversation started? Don't wait until the day of the presentation to start a conversation with an audience; begin the dialogue early.

As you learned in Chapter 6, when you shift your view of presentations from a one-time experience to a long-term relationship, you'll find yourself in conversation with your audience in all the different places where you touch their lives with your ideas.

But once you have a defined event on a specific day, open up the conversation about your live meeting as soon as you book the date on your calendar.

When you grow your followers on Twitter over time, you'll find they're a powerful resource for finding out more about your potential audiences, testing ideas, and conducting research. But even if you're starting from scratch without any Twitter followers yet, you can still do a number of things both online and offline to start the conversation early with your audiences.

Researching your audience

Find your audience on the web and learn about what they're discussing. Start by searching the web using terms your audience is likely using in their discussions about your presentation topic. Use a search engine as well as the Twitter search page at http://search.twitter.com. Look for articles, blog posts, white papers, and Twitter mentions of your topic. Speaker Beth Kanter describes this research process as following "the social media ant trails of my audience," meaning that people leave an online record of their conversations and she tracks these down to learn more about her audience. When she finds example of topics, she'll take a screen capture and include it in her presentation to make the material directly relevant to her audience.

One of the richest sources of information about your audience is the comments section of blog posts, where an author has touched a nerve and triggered a robust discussion. Take the time to read through the posts, where you'll likely identify

- The topics of most interest to your audience.
- People who are passionate about your topic.
- Some of the resources that potential audience members are reading, viewing, and integrating into their work.

If you find a rich vein of conversation about a topic, tap it for the valuable resource that it is.

Inviting your audience to shape your presentation

If you have a blog, you have another rich resource at your fingertips to find out more about your potential audience members. Though all of your blog readers might not be attending your next event, they might still have things on their minds that can be of benefit to your presentation.

Write a post asking your readers what they would like to hear at your next presentation. For example, as social media expert Peter Kim prepared for his panel discussion with Jeremiah Owyang and Charlene Li at the Web 2.0 Expo in April 2009, he posted on his blog the title and description of his session and asked his readers

What would you expect to hear covered in the session?

What questions come to mind that you would want answered?

How can we make it a session that you walk away from satisfied?

The post generated several dozen comments, helping Peter ensure his presentation covered what his audience wanted to learn.

When you build your presentation home page as described in Chapter 6, you create a powerful resource for engaging your audience in advance of your presentation—helping you shape your ideas. Here you can put up rough drafts to prompt discussion, post related articles, and link to in-depth resources you otherwise won't be able to cover during the live event.

Asking your audience's opinion in online surveys

Asking for comments on your blog or Twitter will help you collect free-form and anecdotal information. If you'd like to collect information in a more structured and quantifiable way, try using an online survey tool.

When you set up the survey, aim to get a sense of how interested your audience is in different topics, their levels of knowledge of a topic, and what they would like to hear that you might not yet know about (**Figure 7-5**).

To get as many people as possible to complete the survey, try to keep it no more than one page, intriguing, and to the point.

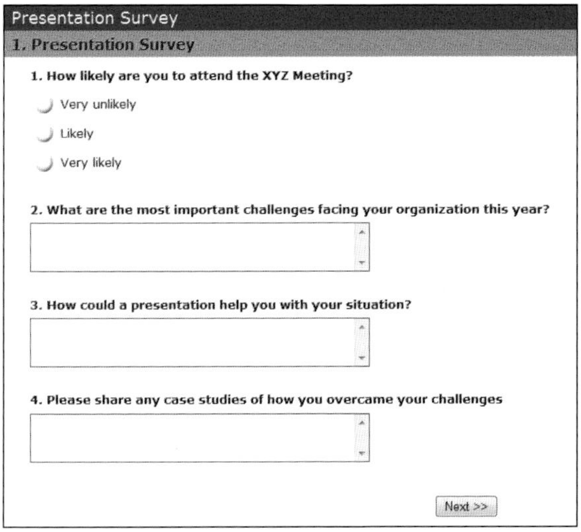

FIGURE 7-5: Use an online tool like SurveyMonkey to poll your audience about their levels of experience and the topics that might be of interest to them.

You'll get some of the best response rates if you coordinate with your host to include a brief online survey as part of the event registration process. Online services such as Eventbrite allow you to add a survey to your event signup page. Otherwise, include a link to the survey in your blog or on Twitter.

Collecting case studies

Use Twitter or a blog post to ask your audience members for practical examples and case studies that demonstrate some of the ideas you'll talk about during your presentation.

For example, author David Meerman Scott put up a blog post asking his readers a question related to his presentation topic: "What are the most difficult issues you face getting your bosses to do social media?" David received several dozen comments on his post, and he used what he learned from those comments to create the opening for his presentation.

During his opening, David asked his audience the same question, and then told a story provided by one of his commenters, describing how she had tried something new with social media and was fired for it. He explained that he understood the obstacles the audience members face with their bosses—showing that he was in touch with their needs and challenges—and then explained ways to overcome the organization's resistance to change yet still keep their bosses happy.

When you collect case studies, be sure to get permission to use the names of individuals and companies; otherwise you should make them generic by removing names and any other identifying information.

Arranging to meet your fans in person

If you already have people who have expressed interest in your work, use social media to arrange to meet them in person. For example, use a blog post or tweet to invite them to a book signing directly after your talk or invite them for a coffee before or a drink after your presentation.

By making a connection with your online fans at an offline, in-person meeting, you can get them excited to spread the good word about your work and your ideas.

Reaching your audience when they are not on blogs or Twitter

Not all of your potential audience members will be reading your blog or following you on Twitter, so you might need to reach out to them in other ways. Speaking coach Olivia Mitchell says, "I think you need to reach them directly by email and even by phone. You can send each audience member an email asking them to click through to a survey on SurveyMonkey—and then you can also phone a few representative audience members to get a more in-depth feel for their needs."

Setting Up for the Backchannel

When you walk into the room of a backchannel presentation, you should already have a number of things in place:

- Thorough knowledge of your audience through research and conversation.
- A framework for your presentation that you'll flesh out with your audience.
- The four tweets you would like your audience to pass on.

Arrive early to set up your equipment and check that the wireless connection is working. Then set up the tools you'll use to engage the backchannel.

Displaying the backchannel details on an introductory slide

When you have your presentation tools set up, display a title slide on the screen that audience members see as they enter the room. Be sure to include at a minimum

- Your session title.
- Your name.
- The Twitter hashtag.
- Your Twitter username.

As shown in **Figure 7-6**, this title slide provides a visual cue that you welcome the backchannel from the start. It encourages people to be in a relationship with you via Twitter if they enjoy your presentation.

FIGURE 7-6:
Display a title slide with your Twitter credentials, among other information, to show you welcome the backchannel.

Using technology to help your audience connect

While your audience is getting settled, try using a tool like the Hello application (**Figure 7-7** on the next page) or A Seat Apart to help them connect with one another. Using these tools, audience members note where they are sitting via Twitter, and then they can search audience members' profiles to see if there's anyone with common interests they'd like to meet. They can also search the audience using names and skill sets.

tip ❯ Find out more about the Hello application at http://hello.carsonified.com and about A Seat Apart at http://aseatapart.getsugarspun.com.

FIGURE 7-7:
The Hello application uses Twitter to help you find other people in the audience who share common interests.

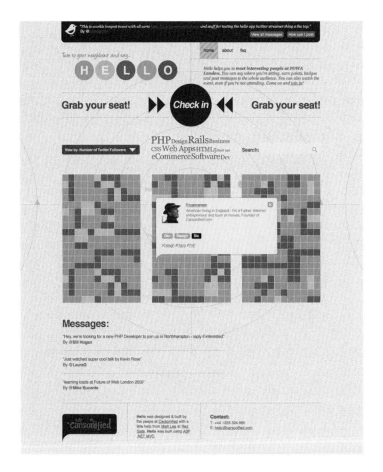

Welcoming the Backchannel as You Begin

With the fundamentals in place, you can now set up a warm welcome for both your online and offline audiences.

Establishing expectations of the presentation

When you stand up to welcome your audience, let them know right away that your presentation is not a lecture—it's a dialogue between them and you.

State that the Law of Two Feet is in effect—that if after giving you a chance they don't think this presentation is a match for them, they are free to leave (so long as they don't distract others). On the other hand, if they think the session is good, they are encouraged to use the backchannel to invite others to attend as well.

Invite your audience to leave their laptops and smart phones open.

Inform them that the details of your presentation—including slides, notes, handouts, and source materials—are available online on your presentation home page.

Making these points at the start should make your audience members in the backchannel feel welcome and at ease.

Explaining the backchannel to those who are not connected

There will always be people in the audience who are not aware of what a backchannel is or how to join in. Make them feel welcome by briefly explaining that part of the audience is using their computers to create a place to have an online conversation during your presentation. Let them know that you welcome use of the backchannel because this tool empowers people to reach outside the room—adding links and comments to the information and also connecting and collaborating with one another.

Welcoming those in the backchannel inside the room

If you're unsure how many people are in the backchannel, or even how many are even aware of the concept, you might want to ask for a show of hands of those participating in the backchannel.

Explain that you'll take periodic breaks to check what's on the minds of those in the backchannel—and you'll let everyone know that's what you're doing. Explain that backchannel comments might provide a springboard for a conversation or for exploring a new topic. In any case, you'll open up the floor to everyone in the room to join the conversation.

Suggesting backchannel guidelines

Display a slide that displays the backchannel ground rules or, at the very least, the Golden Rule of the Backchannel described in Web Appendix C at

www.backchannelbook.com (**Figure 7-8**). This is an especially good idea if you antici-
pate a rowdy audience because of the session topic or audience type.

FIGURE 7-8:
Display the
Backchannel Golden
Rule to make sure
the audience knows
you might read out
loud what they are
writing on Twitter.

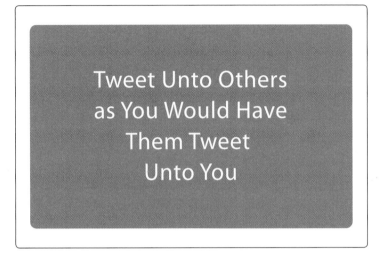

Showing this slide can mitigate any issues that might come up if you choose to read
aloud backchannel comments.

If you are using a more extended backchannel agreement of some sort (see Web
Appendix C), provide a printed version in a meeting handout or a link to an online
version.

Welcoming those in the backchannel outside the room

Be sure to welcome people in the backchannel who are not attending in person, especially if you are video-streaming your presentation. This recognizes their presence and
invites their participation. It also lets the people in the room know that they are not the
only audience members participating in the presentation.

Starting Strong

It's always been important to make a good impression in the first few minutes of a
presentation, but now it's more important than ever because audiences simply won't
wait forever for you to get to your point.

If audience members feel as if you're dawdling, they'll have no problem invoking the Law of Two Feet described in Chapter 4 and Web Appendix C. If you don't get to your point quickly, they'll simply get up and walk out. You have to get to your point quickly so your audience can decide whether they'll stay around to participate.

In order to start fast and strong, consider asking the person who introduces you to welcome the backchannel as described in the previous section. When they do this, it paves the way for you to jump right in and make the powerful impact that you need to make right away.

Getting to the point in the first five slides

You can no longer get away with putting up a slide that lists *Agenda* or *Introduction* at the start of your presentation. Nor can you get away with kicking off your presentation with too many details or a list of your accomplishments. In a world in which your audience is accustomed to high-quality media at their fingertips, you need to capture their attention out of the gate. You must engage your audience within the first five slides or at least the first five minutes of your presentation.

At a minimum, your opening should include the classic elements of story structure as described in Chapter 6:

- The presentation's context and your audience's role in it.
- A challenge they face (Point A).
- Where they want to be (Point B).
- How they get from Point A to Point B.

When you include these elements, you make an emotional connection with your audience, you recognize a problem they face, you explain how your information can empower them to solve it, and you set the action in motion to carry your story forward.

Getting buy-in at the start

An effective way to connect with your audience is to identify a challenge they face. To get early buy-in from your audience, open your conversation with an affirmation that they, in fact, face the very problem to which you provide a solution. To do that, create a simple slide to prompt conversation that will lead to buy-in of your ideas at the start of the presentation.

For example, if your audience is facing new competition in their marketplace, insert a text box on a slide with the word *competition* (**Figure 7-9**). When you advance to this slide, say, "I understand a new competitor has entered your marketplace. What impact do you think this might have?"

FIGURE 7-9:
Prompting conversation right away about a challenge your audience faces affirms you're on track and gets buy-in on the direction of the presentation.

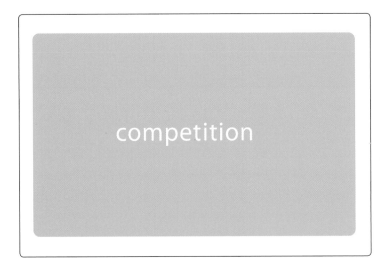

As you pause and listen to what people say, you'll get a good sense here at the start of your presentation what their current feelings are and what they would like to cover.

> **tip ❯** If people are reluctant to respond to the entire group—as they might be at the start of your presentation—ask them a question and have them tell the answer to the person seated next to them. Or, have them answer the question via Twitter. As speaking coach Olivia Mitchell explains, this can work well with large audiences or with people who are not comfortable replying in front of a large group.

As in this example of using only a single word on a slide, the less information on the screen, the better. As you subtract visual information from the screen, you open up more room for conversation.

Involving your audience early and often

You have to take the lead and involve people from the start. Set the example with an activity and don't allow your audience to be passive.

According to speaking and training coach Karen Lawson, when you engage people early, you get them thinking that maybe "this is going to be different. And they will sit up and take notice. If you lose them up front, it's harder to get them later. Have them doing something in the first few minutes."

Taking at Least Three Twitter breaks

Your audience in the backchannel really does want to be involved in a conversation with you, and the best way to do that is to pause for backchannel discussion breaks. Blogger Robert Scoble sometimes takes Twitter breaks every 15 minutes to get immediate feedback from his audience about how things are going and learn about questions, suggestions, and new insights.

As described in Chapter 6, when you structure your presentation in at least three sections around your three supporting tweets, you create the opportunity to involve your audience at the end of each section. You should involve them a minimum of three times within a typical 45-minute presentation.

Displaying a Twitter break slide

Once you're ready to take a Twitter break, announce the break as you display a slide (**Figure 7-10**) that designates the break and also reminds your audience of the backchannel access information. Be sure to inform them of the length of the Twitter break both visually (on the slide itself) and verbally (tell them).

FIGURE 7-10: When you take a Twitter break, display a slide that reminds your audience of the backchannel access information.

Reinforcing each of your three supporting tweets

Another benefit of a Twitter break is that it provides you with an opportunity to rein-force whichever one of the three supporting tweets that corresponds with the section of your presentation you just completed. After you display your Twitter break slide, return to a slide with the tweet that summarizes the first section of your presentation (**Figure 7-11**). This reinforces your point and keeps the conversation focused until your break is finished and you move on to the next point.

FIGURE 7-11:
After you've displayed your Twitter break slide, advance to a slide that summarizes the tweet that corresponds to the previous section.

Introducing a moderator

It's difficult to handle the job of public speaking while simultaneously remaining aware of what people are saying in the backchannel. You run the risk of neglecting your talk or becoming distracted by the backchannel. To manage this more effectively, assign someone to moderate the backchannel—either somebody you know or a tweeting audience member.

Be sure to discuss with moderators in advance what criteria you would like them to use to select backchannel comments. As moderators review comments from the back-channel, they must determine if there are any relevant questions, concerns, or general comments you need to know about (more on this in Chapter 8).

tip ❯ If you don't have a moderator, you can review the Twitterstream yourself on a laptop or smartphone. Events expert Jeff Hurt sets up an extra monitor on the floor facing speakers that displays the backchannel so speakers don't have to use a laptop or smartphone.

Reviewing the Twitterstream together

Explain to the audience that you'll be reviewing the Twitterstream together and also opening the floor to verbal Q&A for those who are not participating in the backchannel. If you don't have a moderator, scan the backchannel comments yourself with your audience. Select a comment to read to the whole audience and then address it (**Figure 7-12**).

FIGURE 7-12: Speaker Olivia Mitchell addresses backchannel comments with her audience.
(Photo courtesy of Olivia Mitchell)

Olivia Mitchell found that when she had many people tweeting during a presentation

There were far too many questions/comments for me to address during a Twitter break, but I noticed some had been re-tweeted so I addressed those first. Building on this, you could encourage the audience to re-tweet the questions they're most interested in.

Displaying the Backchannel During Twitter Breaks

To prepare to display the backchannel during your presentation

- Connect your computer to a projector that will display your desktop on a screen in the room. You likely already have this set up if you plan to use presentation software.
- Open up whatever application you'll use to display the backchannel (visit www.backchannelbook.com for a list of at least a dozen tools you can use for displaying backchannels).
- Click Alt+Tab on a PC to switch from your presentation software (or other application) to the backchannel application and share it on the projector screen for all to see.
- When you're done sharing the backchannel, click Alt+Tab again to return to your presentation software.

Alternatively, use a tool that displays Twitter within the slides of your presentation software so you don't have to toggle between screens.

Involving those in the room not in the backchannel

After you've shared a backchannel comment or two, open up the floor to verbal questions from those who are not participating in the backchannel.

In keeping with the informal style of backchannel presentations, it's good practice to pass a microphone around the room (with help from staff or volunteers if it's a large room) rather than to place a fixed microphone stand in the middle of the room that people have to line up to use.

Involving people outside the room

Extend the dialogue to the much larger audience by taking questions from people in the backchannel who are outside the room. As you scan through the backchannel comments, look for any that identify whether someone is from outside the room or outside the country, and share the comment and the location of the commenter with the rest of the group. This makes everyone feel a part of the much broader community that the backchannel invites and creates.

Making sure nobody feels left out

Both you and the moderator should make sure you stay fully aware that you're including everyone in the dialogue. Don't let a vocal minority take over the conversation and move it in a direction you didn't want to go.

In all cases, be sure to open up the floor and ask if anyone would like to say something. Invite them to tweet their thoughts if they don't otherwise feel comfortable sharing them with the group.

Wrapping up the Twitter break

When you've used up your allotted time—say, five minutes—bring your audience's attention back to the topic at hand by summarizing where you are at this point and where you are headed next in the presentation. It's up to you to make the smooth transition from your previous section, through the backchannel conversation, and on to your next point.

Automating Your Involvement in the Backchannel

As described in an earlier section, because you're likely focusing on speaking to your audience, your ability as a presenter to join the backchannel discussion as it happens is very limited. But, just as technology is creating more streams of information than you can manage, it can also help you solve this problem by automating the way you participate.

Auto tweeting your key points

One way to insert your thoughts directly into the backchannel is to give your moderator or an assistant access to your Twitter account, and ask him or her to send each of your four tweets when you reach each tweet during your presentation.

Another way is to use a tool like SocialOomph (formerly called Tweetlater) to send automated tweets during your presentation. With this service, you set up your tweets in advance of your presentation and set the timing for them to be posted at any time intervals you choose.

By tweeting your own posts, you ensure the accuracy of your points, make it easy for your audience to simply re-tweet the posts you sent, and you leave the impression that you're a very savvy backchannel presenter.

Integrating Twitter into Keynote presentation software

Keynote Tweet is a free software application that works with Keynote presentation software (not with PowerPoint) and publishes Twitter posts automatically as you give your presentation. After setting up the software, in the slide notes area you type the text that you want Keynote Tweet to tweet when you advance to a particular slide. When you advance to that slide, the Keynote Tweet sends the text to Twitter for you.

If you've created your slides using complete sentences as headlines (as recommended in Chapter 6), you could add your headlines to the notes section of the slides you choose and send your slide headlines as tweets.

A tool like this ensures the timing of your tweets is accurate because they don't go out until you advance your slides.

Integrating Twitter into PowerPoint

Timo Elliott created a suite of free tools (www.sapweb20.com/blog/powerpoint-twitter-tools) that integrate PowerPoint and Twitter, allowing you to

- Display a Twitter ticker bar at the bottom of slides that searches a hashtag.
- Display a feedback slide with questions and comments from Twitter.
- Conduct real-time voting over Twitter.

Expect to see more tools like these emerge as presenters find creative ways to use Twitter to engage their audiences.

Involving Your Audience Using Twitter and the Web

Be sure to make full use of Twitter and the web during your presentation. The act of Twittering itself gives audiences something to do, and you can make what they do even more useful by guiding them a bit with their computer mice and keyboards.

Asking a Twitter question

Make effective use of Twitter by asking your audience a question. Then ask them to post their answers on Twitter along with the meeting's hashtag.

For example, request that people on Twitter post their three favorite resources on your topic, and then review these resources in the Twitterstream and share the best ones with the group.

According to consultant Nancy White, "If you ask your audience a juicy question, you'll get engagement." So give your audiences something to talk about.

Don't ask a question for the sake of asking one to build engagement; spend time choosing your questions well so you really stimulate the minds of your audience members and get the intellectual sparks flying.

Polling your audience

Consider a live poll to see how you're doing and whether you need to make adjustments to your material.

If you'd like to use Twitter as a tool to take a poll, there are resources such as Twtpoll that help you set up a poll very quickly and easily.

But if asking people to raise their hands or verbally respond to take a quick poll works faster and more efficiently than asking people to take a Twitter poll, by all means try that instead.

Giving your audience an online challenge to complete

Tapping into your audience's ability to collectively explore a topic is a marvelous, new, and untapped resource.

If you set up the task in the right way, you'll be able to harness the collective brainpower of the group to accomplish something they otherwise would not be able to do alone.

For example, give your audience something to do online—a brief research project, a puzzle to solve, or even a clue to uncover somewhere on your presentation home page.

Offering source materials

Let people know where they can get additional information that you described during your presentation.

For example, you'll likely have only enough time to share an overview of a case study during your presentation, even though there are many more juicy details to tell. Let your audience know where to find the additional information—likely on your presentation home page.

To make your offer of more resources even more compelling, ask your audience to find a certain detail within a resource. For example, offer a free copy of a book or a gift certificate to the first person who finds and tweets the item.

Focusing the Attention of the Backchannel

On occasion you might find it helpful to use audience participation in the room in a way that shuts down laptops, focuses attention on an important topic, and creates an experience your audience long remembers.

Involving your audience with one another

Karen Lawson recommends a range of techniques to get audiences involved, but the most powerful ones involve the audience engaging one another. According to Karen, "Some people think interaction means between audience and speaker (like Q&A). But true interaction is among the people in the audience." Involving your audience gives them a way to participate and to share their own stories.

Karen teaches a technique she calls *active knowledge sharing* that begins with something she wants to teach. For example, she teaches the point that people process spoken words at a speed that is different than the speed at which they process written words. She asks the audience to fill in the blanks of sentences, such as: *A speaker speaks at a rate of ____ words per minute. A reader reads at a rate of ____ words per minute.* Then she asks the audience to turn to their neighbors or break into small groups to work together to come up with the numbers. (For this exercise, the audience is not to look up the answers on the Internet; they are to come up with their best guesses.)

Karen walks around to see what people write, or asks a few groups to share their answers. Then she reveals the answers. When she structures an exercise this way, people really want to know the answer because she sets it up as a puzzle to be solved—that engages them.

A similar exercise is to assign a task related to your audience's professions. Pair people with their neighbors and give them five minutes to complete the task; then ask them to report back to the group. The responsibility of delivering something to the group focuses their attention and builds relationships with other people in the audience.

Walking into the room

When there is a backchannel in a room, audience members can easily become distracted by their laptop or smartphone screens. To refocus attention and reinforce your most important ideas, consider walking into the room.

In his book *Working the Room* (Harvard Business School Press, 2003), presentation coach Nick Morgan describes how much the rise of radio and television changed the expectations of audiences, who quickly got used to having television personalities in the intimate space of their living rooms. He explains:

> *Our speaking styles have indeed become more conversational, but speakers in public spaces haven't learned to deliver the physical closeness that mirrors the linguistic closeness on television.*

Since so many presenters tend to stay at the front of the room and pace back and forth between the podium and screen, Nick recommends re-creating the experience people have with presenters on television by walking into the audience during the key points of your presentation.

He recommends you divide the audience into quadrants and "find an audience member, move toward that person, deliver the point, and then move away."

The distance you stand from an audience member is important—Nick describes four distinct zones revealed by research:

> *Twelve feet or more is public space. From twelve feet to four feet is social space. From four feet to a foot and a half is personal space. And, in most Western cultures, less than a foot and a half is intimate space.*

To create the personal relationship people expect from presenters on television, Nick recommends that public speaking take place within personal space so that "when you get to the most important line, I want you to be four feet or less (but not closer than a foot and a half) from that person."

Speaker David Meerman Scott follows Nick's advice and walks out in the audience three times, at the three most important parts of his presentation—the introductory questions for his audience, the section that talks about a crucial point he wants to make, and his closing call to action.

According to David, this creates physicality in a live presentation that can never be transferred in video. And importantly, it focuses the attention of the backchannel.

> **tip ❯** What are the three times you would walk out into the room during your next presentation? Whatever they are, build them from the hierarchy you created in Chapter 7, so that your speech, your verbal metaphor, the screen, your handouts, and your body movement all work together to emphasize your most important points.

Creating a human bar chart

Speaker Jared Spool created a particularly innovative exercise called the Human Bar Chart to bring to life the often static nature of his PowerPoint data charts. As audience members walk into the room for his presentations related to market research, he asks volunteers from the audience to complete a survey inspired by a Gallup poll that measures their feelings about a set of national brand names on a scale from –11 to 11. He has placed individual signs with the brand names on the wall, each with a number corresponding with the same scale.

When he brings up the topic of displaying market research data, he announces a brand name and asks the volunteers to come to the wall and stand at the numbered sign where they rated the brand. If it's a popular brand, the bodies of people standing at the signs usually create a bell curve, usually to the right of 0. Then he announces a different brand that is less popular, and the entire group shifts over to the left.

As he announces another set of popular and unpopular brands, the participants shift from one side to another. Sometimes those who strongly prefer one brand also strongly dislike its competing brand. Jared interviews individuals about their feelings as they switch back and forth against the wall as they change position on the scale.

The result? According to Jared, "It makes it a human moment and makes the data about people rather than statistics." He spends 12 to 15 minutes on the exercise because it teaches some important lessons, and people remember the event for months, even years afterward. But Jared says he wouldn't do it for every presentation every time because "If every point had it, all the theatrics would turn into noise, so you have to choose it judiciously."

Visually improvising

Another type of exercise that always shuts down the laptops is visual improv. The speaker displays a PowerPoint presentation on the wall in which there is one simple photo object on each slide (**Figure 7-13**), and each slide is timed to automatically advance after 30 seconds.

FIGURE 7-13:
The visual improv exercise focuses all eyes on each person in the room in turn.

The speaker begins with the first image on the screen, and uses the image to improvise the beginning of a story while the image is onscreen. After 30 seconds the image changes to the next, and then a new member of the audience stands up, looks at the new image, and uses it as a prompt to continue to improvise the story. After 30 seconds the image changes, and the next audience member continues to improvise the story. The group continues the story going around the room for about six to eight minutes.

Several interesting things happen. The audience is wholly focused on the experience—no one is typing because their turn is coming up, plus they are looking forward to seeing what the next person will say. Laughter fills the room because of the creative improvisations. And the audience experiences a powerful lesson about how presentations can actually be an act of audience creation rather than only presenter creation.

> **tip ❯** For step-by-step instructions on how to create a visual improv exercise yourself, see Chapter 11 on the CD of my book *Beyond Bullet Points* (Microsoft Press, 2007).

Wrapping Up

In addition to making a strong conclusion to your presentation, consider ways you can grow your Twitter followers from among the audience members in the room as you wrap things up.

Including your Twitter address on your final slide

Be sure to include your Twitter address on your final slide to make it as easy as possible for people to follow you if they liked your presentation. You might also include your email address and phone number if you would like for people to reach you through those means.

Offering a copy of your presentation

If you'd like to grow your email list so you can keep in touch with your audience members, ask for their business cards and let them know you'll email a copy of your presentation to them if they agree to opt-in to your list. If you'd like to grow your blog readership, let your audience know you'll post a link to the materials there. Or to grow your followers on Twitter, let your audience know that you'll send out a link to the slides—or even offer bonus content—via a tweet.

Checking Your Results in the Twitterstream

Before the backchannel became available, if your audience agreed or disagreed with you, they might complete a speaker feedback form or tell a few people during the break. But now your audience is posting from the start of the presentation to the end, providing you with more feedback than you could dream possible. Here in the Twitterstream, you'll find an extended commentary on your ideas and your delivery.

As you will learn in Chapter 8, you have to take feedback with a grain of salt and sort out the useful comments from the ones you can't do anything about. The amount of feedback might be overwhelming at first—especially if you're not used to it. To make it easier to read all of the tweets, print the tweets and highlight the ones you find most relevant. As you get used to scanning the Twitterstream over time, you'll quickly be able to find the most useful material you want to address.

Panning for nuggets of gold in the Twitterstream

Probably one of the most surprising things you'll find is that that your audience will pick up on an idea that you didn't think was important.

Speaker Simon Young wrote about his recent experience as a speaker, saying "It was also great to go back over the tweets sent during my presentation, afterwards. I could see where I confused people, where people got excited, and which phrases were the most re-tweetable. Priceless feedback!"

Since you're always immersed in your ideas, it is really hard to step back and really see things the way your audience sees them, especially from their different perspectives, backgrounds, and personalities.

Your audience might pick up on a thought you didn't consider important and then they might tweet it. Then, you'll be surprised to find out that someone else in the audience re-tweeted it so that others could read it. Then you might find that that people all over Twitter have re-tweeted the original thought, reaching thousands more people outside the room.

In this example, the huge value of the Twitterstream is that the backchannel corrected your idea of what you thought was important to your audience and they let you know what really worked for them. In your next presentation, you can take the new idea and run with it—even making it center stage, if necessary.

Archiving your Twitterstream

Whether you use Twitter or another tool for a backchannel, be sure to copy the tweets from your audience members and save them to a safe location.

Archive the conversation on your presentation home page, along with additional resource materials you choose to provide from the presentation. Additionally, you can subscribe to an RSS feed of a Twitter search of your hashtag to keep track of post-presentation conversations on Twitter.

Keeping the Twitterstream honest

Of course, just as presenters aren't perfect, neither are audience members. So you'll want to review your Twitterstream to make sure the feedback is factually correct.

Just be aware of what people write about you. If there's miscommunication or a misunderstanding, quickly post a correction or clarification.

Continuing the Backchannel Conversation

Don't let the conversation end when the applause does. Reach out afterward and continue what you started during your presentation.

Once you've had a chance to review the Twitterstream, write a more extended post about the comments in your blog. Include the best posts, along with any themes or unanswered questions that emerged.

Use the backchannel to thank your audience for their time; let them know how much you enjoyed being with them.

Follow up on any other open items from your presentation, and when you get a tweet, you can continue the conversation on Twitter or move on to more extended conversation by email, phone, or in person.

To keep the conversation going, ask your audience for any additional resources they might have or present some open-ended questions to keep people talking. It might be that others have posted about your presentation on their blogs; search for those blogs and join the conversation there.

As you get to know your audience, you'll pinpoint your backchannel hubs—those who are particularly excited about your ideas, and then you can reach out to them after the presentation to keep in touch.

After all, when your presentation ends, the relationship—and conversation—is only just beginning.

Handling Instant Feedback from the Backchannel

Practice a range of scenarios to
become better prepared to handle
instant (and sometimes negative) feedback
from the backchannel

There have certainly always been comments about presentations shared among any group of audience members, but until now those thoughts have been confined to private thoughts, evaluation forms, and perhaps hallway discussions.

Now, with the click of a mouse, those same thoughts are published immediately, read by others inside the room and out, and amplified in attention and impact.

According to South by Southwest Interactive Festival director Hugh Forrest:

> *Technologies such as Twitter allow real-time communication in a way that was never before possible. So, the feedback loop no longer starts 30 minutes after the presentation is over—or even 5 minutes after the talk is over. The feedback is instantaneous and it is usually brutally honest. In the best-case scenario, such immediacy will provide even more incentive for presenters to put together dynamic presentations (as opposed to thinking that they can kind of BS their way through the lecture—which unfortunately is something that would happen far too often in the pre-Twitter conference landscape).*

Though often the feedback will be positive, the comments you get will sometimes be negative—as Hugh describes, "brutally honest." And these negative comments wield power that can potentially disrupt your presentation.

The introduction of instantaneous feedback is an important new phenomenon that a backchannel introduces to live presentations, and it's essential to plan for how you're going to handle both negative and positive feedback at your next presentation.

The Power of Negative Backchannel Feedback

According to psychologist Jaine Fraser, "People are less likely to disagree with someone who has made a negative comment than with someone who's made a positive one, especially if there have been two or more negative comments."

Sometimes simply posting a comment serves as a pressure release valve that lets out pent-up negative emotion. Just tweeting a negative thought might be enough for people to get emotions off their chests, and then they're done with it.

But other times the negativity can continue to build until it leads to a blowup of the types described in Chapter 4. When negative builds upon negative in such a fast-moving environment (usually while a presenter is unaware of what is happening), it's all too easy for an audience to cross a line from being dissatisfied to becoming an unruly Twitter mob.

Hugh Forrest cites an example:

> For instance, suppose three or four people in Panel Room A begin to tweet about how much they dislike the presentation. Do their tweets influence the perception of others to have a negative opinion of that session or that networking party or that event? I hope not. But, I do think we are often swayed by the opinions of others ("if everyone else thinks this panel is lame, then I guess I think it is bad also"). So, I have some concerns that the tweet mob can gain its own bully pulpit... and thereby gain too much influence over the tone/theme/vibe of an event.

Because of the large influence negative comments can have, it's important to handle them proactively.

Neutralizing Negativity and Snowballing Positivity

Obviously the most effective way to plan for negative comments is to do everything you can to prevent them from happening in the first place. You've already gone to great lengths to do that in previous chapters to create a solid structure for your ideas, to ensure a high level of participation, to write a clear session description, and to allow the Law of Two Feet to be in force so people are only at your presentation because they want to be.

Calling out positive comments about your ideas

One thing you can do to potentially neutralize negativity is to build a dynamic where positive comments build from one another in a snowball effect.

As you or the moderator view the comments in the backchannel, seek out comments that make a positive contribution to the conversation. For example, share comments with the larger group that enhance points you're making or offer good suggestions that you did not mention (**Figure 8-1** on the next page).

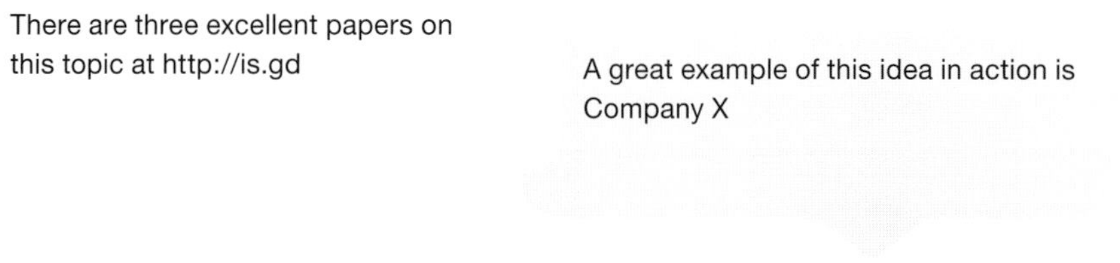

FIGURE 8-1:
Look for positive
comments in the
Twitterstream
that you can share
with the rest of the
audience.

There are three excellent papers on
this topic at http://is.gd

A great example of this idea in action is
Company X

When you find positive comments you'd like to share, call out the names of the audience members, ask them to raise their hands, read the comments, and then thank
them for their contributions.

Promoting Backchannel Tools That Are Not Anonymous

As you learned in Chapter 2, some backchannel tools such as chat rooms
allow their users to remain anonymous. When commenters are anonymous
and are not personally held accountable for the comments they make, the tone
of the backchannel is often negative. Although you can't control what tools
people use, you can work with hosts to promote backchannel tools that are
not anonymous. Event organizer Pete Reilly suggests that hosts provide "some
other incentive to be on there (prizes for most comments, most 'favorited'
comment, most helpful to the conference, best criticism without snark, and
so on). That won't eliminate the snarkiness or other backchannels, but if there
is a smaller audience, the snark will be more limited."

Recognizing positive comments creates a welcoming atmosphere in the room, encour-
ages more positivity in the backchannel, and creates some really happy audience
members who will spread the good feelings to their followers far and wide.

Ignoring positive comments about you or your delivery

Of course, when you seek comments to share with the room, don't call out the ones
that would sound as if they are self-serving. Examples of these include comments that
compliment you or your ideas (**Figure 8-2**). Reading these sounds like you're self-
promoting—ignore them and let them speak for themselves.

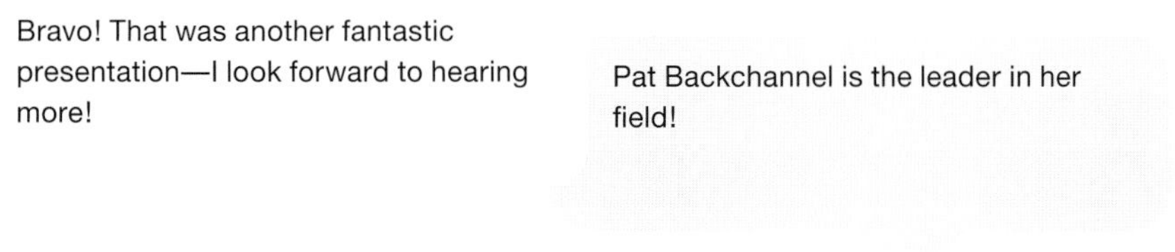

Bravo! That was another fantastic presentation—I look forward to hearing more!

Pat Backchannel is the leader in her field!

FIGURE 8-2:
Ignore the positive comments that would create the impression that you are self-serving.

But in spite of all you do to neutralize negativity before it happens, you will still hear negative comments from the backchannel and elsewhere. The crucial question is, "How will you deal with them?"

Preparing Yourself for Negative Backchannel Feedback

The first thing to do is to prepare yourself mentally by taking a positive perspective on how you view backchannel feedback.

Consultant Sacha Chua describes how she engaged the backchannel during a panel discussion:

> *Thanks to Twitter, I could tell that people were dissatisfied with the slow and moderated online questions process, skeptical of the event and the speakers, and interested in engaging further. I announced that I'd be watching the Twitter backchannel, and during our panel, I kept an eye on the questions and comments that flowed past. That let me shape what I said to incorporate other people's perspectives and points of view, and that totally rocked.*

As Sacha demonstrated in this example, the backchannel is a valuable tool for you to use to truly listen to any comments, learn and make adjustments as needed to improve your skills, and do a better job of choosing material to present to your audiences. If you speak during a panel discussion or in another free-form format, you have more flexibility to adapt to feedback. If you deliver a prepared presentation, prepare additional material in case you decide to change course and tackle a new issue your audience wants to hear more about.

Don't take backchannel criticism personally, but rather look at the feedback as a way to continue to sharpen your skills and become a better communicator. Consultant Nancy White says, "Positive and negative feedback, even heckling (which was and still is used in some contexts and cultures)—if we pay attention to it—improves us as speakers. "

Speaker Jared Spool draws from his background in theater to put criticism in context, explaining that no matter how many positive reviews a performer receives, if you get a single negative one, you sink emotionally. But if you are the type of person who decides to stand in front of other people and present, you care about what people think. According to Jared, "If you don't care what people think, you're probably not good at what you do."

Should You Ignore or Call Out Negative Comments?

So when you or your moderators come across a negative comment from someone in the backchannel, what do you do?

To make the question practical, put yourself in a scenario where you are giving a presentation where there is a backchannel. Your talk has been going well so far, at least until you decided to take your second Twitter break. As you scan through the backchannel comments, you see that someone made a negative comment (**Figure 8-3**).

FIGURE 8-3:
What would you do if you faced a scenario where someone said you were not delivering what you promised?

This presentation is not delivering what was promised in the session description

What would you do? Ignore the comment? Or bring it up before the whole group?

Before you decide, the first thing to do is to take a mental pause and detach from your initial emotions. Assess the situation and decide what to do.

When to ignore a negative comment

Your first option is to ignore a negative comment altogether.

Speaking coach Olivia Mitchell says, "You don't have to respond to every negative tweet. If it's a silly comment without any substance, others will recognize it as such and there's no need to draw attention to it. "

You can generally ignore a negative comment (**Figure 8-4**) when

- Engaging the comment would distract you from your objectives for the presentation.
- It is off-topic.
- You can't do anything about it.
- Your emotions are running high, and you don't feel you'll be able to handle the situation well.
- The comment represents the opinion of one or a few people rather than many in the audience.

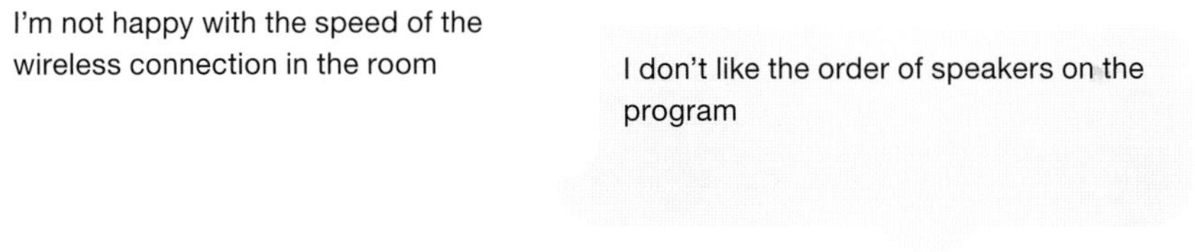

I'm not happy with the speed of the wireless connection in the room

I don't like the order of speakers on the program

FIGURE 8-4:
Ignore comments that you can't do anything about.

When you read a comment and it meets these criteria, simply ignore it and continue on with your presentation.

But in the case of the original scenario in Figure 8-3, instead of ignoring the comment, you might consider calling it out.

When to call out a negative comment

There are instances when you might choose not to ignore a negative comment, but rather to bring it to the attention of the entire audience.

According to Olivia Mitchell, "The ethics of dealing with criticism on Twitter are still evolving, so you want to take it out of the Twitter space and into the live space. That way, people are more likely to abide by the accepted rules of respect for other people."

I'm not following the point here—is anybody else as lost as I am?

RT: I'm not following the point here—is anybody else as lost as I am?

You might want to call out a negative comment (**Figure 8-5**) when

- You feel it represents the opinion of many people in the audience. You can get a sense of this by observing if there are multiple comments in the same vein or re-tweets of the original comment.

- The commenter is distracting other members of the backchannel or disrupting your presentation.

- You determine through the body language of the audience that the tone and mood of the room has turned sour or hostile.

- You can do something about it. For example, a comment represents a misunderstanding or misstatement of fact you can quickly clear up.

- You feel you need to protect or defend your reputation.

How to call out a negative comment

After pausing and reflecting on the situation and deciding to address the comment, be hyper-aware of keeping your emotions under control and the tone of the room positive. Bringing a negative comment out into the open is a potentially risky situation if you or the author of the comment has emotions running high—the perfect conditions for a backchannel blowup.

According to Olivia, there a couple of ways to handle calling out a negative tweet:

1. *Let the audience know that there have been some tweets unhappy about the direction of the presentation. Read them out loud. Then ask the tweeters to elaborate on their concerns. Once you have the full picture, address their concerns.*

   OR

2. *Let the audience know that there have been some tweets unhappy about the direction of the presentation. Ask the audience by show of hands whether they want you to address the concerns or whether they want you to carry on with your presentation as planned. If a large majority wants you to carry on, then do so. The tweeters*

will have seen that they were a small minority and will therefore be likely to accept the decision. However, if a significant group (they might still be a minority—say 20 to 30 percent of the audience) want you to address the issues—then do so.

In the original example in this section, you might say, "There's a comment in the backchannel that this presentation is not delivering what was promised in the session description. I see it's from John Smith—John, could you explain what you mean?" Or, "I've seen a couple of backchannel comments that the presentation is not delivering what was promised in the session description. Please raise your hands if you agree with that point. It looks like about a third of you agree. Could you explain what you mean?"

In this example, if you realize you have strayed from your session description, adjust course and get back on track. Or if it turned out there was a misunderstanding about the session description (or a misprint), you might give permission to those who are finding a mismatch to leave the session if it would not disrupt the presentation.

A Backchannel Feedback Glossary

The act of criticizing a speaker using the backchannel has developed its own vocabulary—some of the words and phrases include

- *Tweckling*: A combination of the words *tweeting* and *heckling*; refers to the act of heckling someone in a Twitter backchannel.
- *Twitterlashing*: Similar to tweckling, it refers to using Twitter to direct critical comments toward a speaker.
- *Harshtags*: The creation of hashtags included in a Twitter post that criticize a speaker, such as #keynotefail.
- *Twitterjacking*: To take control of a presentation by making a comment intended provoke a speaker or other audience members.
- *Snark bomb*: Snark combines the words *snide* and *remark*; refers to a situation when a backchannel expresses negativity that negatively affects an event.

And sometimes you might revisit your response to a comment based on feedback from the larger audience. In one instance, speaker Jared Spool read in a backchannel comment that he should cut back on the comedy he uses in his presentations. He announced to the audience that he received the feedback and planned to cut back on the comedy—but then other audience members booed because they disagreed, and he kept in the comedy.

If it's appropriate, at any point you might tell the commenter you would prefer to talk to the person individually after the presentation out of courtesy and respect for the rest of the audience.

However you resolve the situation, keep the discussion about the negative comment as short as possible and move on.

Practicing Backchannel Feedback Scenarios

Since so much about presenting to a backchannel is new, set aside time to practice scenarios that put you in a range of difficult backchannel situations. The worst thing you can do is wait until a live presentation to decide what you'll do. Instead, spend up-front time rehearsing scenarios in which you deal with a range of comments.

The following situations are based on real-life backchannel experiences. They might never happen to you, but by putting thought into them in advance of a presentation you increase your general confidence, preparedness, and sense of relaxation.

To practice the scenarios, read them to yourself and consider what you would do. Or, invite your colleagues to role-play different backchannel audience members as you rehearse a range of difficult scenarios such as the following.

> **tip >** Visit www.backchannelbook.com to see how other people would respond to these scenarios.

There is not a "right" answer to these scenarios. What you do will depend on you, your audiences, and your specific situations.

Scenario: "You're not listening to us"

In February 2008, the Minnesota Society of Professional Journalists and Minnesota Public Radio hosted a forum on the impact of new media on mainstream media. People who were live-blogging and using Twitter were expecting a discussion rather than a lecture and grew disappointed. According to attendee Greg Swan, "Following the forum, there was all sorts of dust-up—mostly caused by unrealized expectations set by the panel's topic, the format in how the speakers interacted with the audience, and the availability and use of digital backchannels."

Greg was also at the SXSW Interactive Festival in 2008 in the Social Marketing Strategies Metrics panel, where audience members in the backchannel grew frustrated that the presentation was not delivering what had been promised. After an audience member shared his dissatisfaction, he was rebuffed by the moderator. According to Greg, one audience member then posted, "'OK, all together now...let's raise our hands on the count of...three', and people really did raise their hands all across the room. The reporter from the local Austin newspaper looked shocked. Then it got out of hand... Suddenly literally one-tenth of the room started coughing intermittently...for the rest of the panel."

In these cases, the backchannel made it clear that the presenters were not listening or not delivering as advertised (**Figure 8-6**).

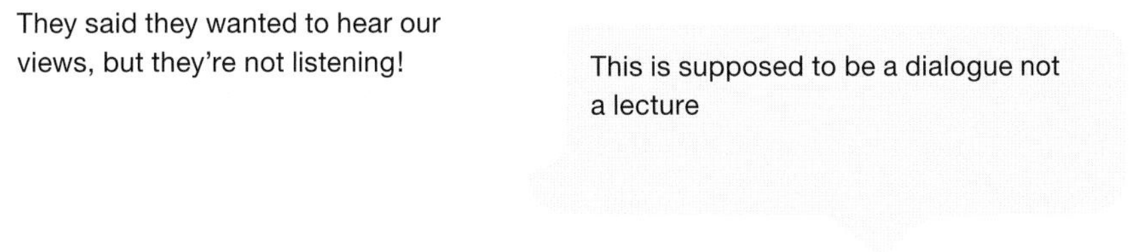

They said they wanted to hear our views, but they're not listening!

This is supposed to be a dialogue not a lecture

FIGURE 8-6:
What would you do if you read comments that said you weren't listening to your audience?

What would you do if you read tweets like these?

Issues to consider include whether the comments represent a large part of the audience, and how disruptive the backchannel is being.

Scenario: "Your facts are wrong or misleading"

In his book *We the Media*, Dan Gillmor describes live-blogging from the PC Forum in Phoenix in 2002 when the CEO of Qwest, Joe Nacchio, got on stage and described the difficulties of raising capital for his company. After receiving a tip from a reader, Dan posted a link to a web page "showing that Nacchio had cashed in more than $200 million in stock while his company's stock price was heading downhill." Fellow blogger Doc Searls also posted the link, then some other audience members in the room read the post, and "around that point, the audience turned hostile," wrote Esther Dyson, whose company, Edventure Holdings, held the conference.

As Gillmor demonstrated, the backchannel is extremely aware of the information a speaker is presenting, and with a browser and wireless connection in hand, they can check your facts in short order.

If the backchannel discovers something that's off, they will shine the light on it and confront presenters with the newly transparent information or otherwise question their credibility (**Figure 8-7**).

FIGURE 8-7:
What would you do if you read comments that said you had your facts wrong?

> She has her facts completely wrong—see http://is.gd

> Here's the information the speaker doesn't want you to know http://is.gd

What would you do if you read tweets like these?

Issues to consider include the importance of maintaining credibility with your audience and clearing up misunderstandings.

Scenario: "Your material is a mismatch for us"

In February 2009, a group of audience members attending an American Society of Association Executives (ASAE) online conference used Twitter to research and refute outdated information that some of the presenters were providing. Caught off guard by the extensive live-tweeting that was undermining the credibility of the event, ASAE eventually learned of what had happened and soon adopted an active social media strategy at its events.

In instances like this, the backchannel will make it clear that the speaker's content is a mismatch with the audience (**Figure 8-8**). The backchannel is also very aware of whether presenters reflect the backgrounds and interests of the audience and will make it known if there is a mismatch, as well as point out if there are gender or demographic imbalances on speaker panels.

FIGURE 8-8:
What would you do if you read comments that said your material was not a good fit for your audience?

> This material is 5 years out of date

> What were they thinking when they selected this topic?

What would you do if you read tweets like these?

Issues to consider include a determination of how many people are unhappy, and whether you have alternate material to present.

Scenario: "Your material is boring"

It's not all that uncommon for audiences to experience boredom, but the backchannel makes the feeling very visible for all to see.

Audience members in the backchannel have a low tolerance for boredom; they expect presenters to get to the point quickly. Audience members express their frustration, in their own words on blog posts and comments, that they are "resentful because they are trapped," that they "suffer in silence," and that they "hate being captive in an audience."

They also express disappointment if they didn't learn much from a presentation or if they are angry because their time was wasted (**Figure 8-9**).

> I'm bored out of my mind—is he seriously going to read all his slides?

> This sucks—I should've gone to the other presentation

FIGURE 8-9:
What would you do if your audience said your presentation was boring?

What would you do if you read tweets like these?

Issues to consider include finding out how many audience members share the sentiment and whether you can do something about the situation.

Scenario: "You made me mad"

Chapter 4 described a range of backchannel blowups that stirred up emotions from audience members—and presenters.

Anything a presenter says is fodder for reaction from audience members—just as it has always been. But now the backchannel provides a way for those strong feelings to be known to a much larger audience both inside and outside a room (**Figure 8-10** on the next page).

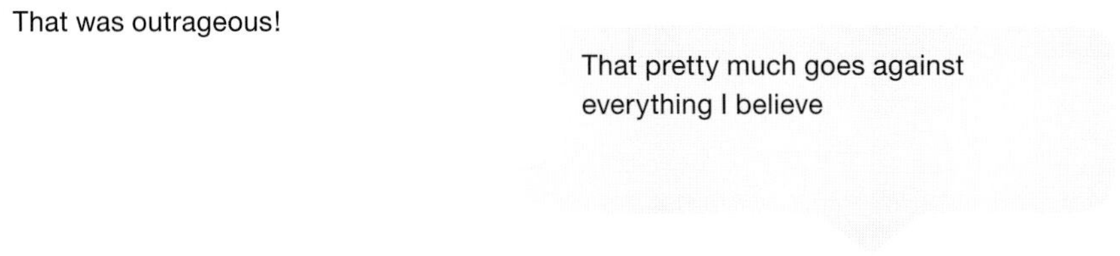

FIGURE 8-10:
What would you
do if you read a
comment from
someone who was
very angry with you?

That was outrageous!

That pretty much goes against
everything I believe

What would you do if you read tweets like these?

Issues to consider include whether the comments represent just one person or are perhaps the feelings of many. Also consider whether you can engage the situation without your own emotions running so high that the presentation goes off track.

Keeping the Presentation on Track

Simply reading through these scenarios begins to prepare you for the comments that the backchannel might introduce to your next presentation. These types of experiences have happened where there are backchannels, and even if you choose to ignore negative comments, at least you will have thought in advance about what you can do.

As you take time to think through the possibilities, to practice scenarios, and to get real-world experience, you'll become more confident at dealing with them.

And as you get good at handling instant feedback, your presentations will become much more dynamic and responsive to the fast-moving backchannel experience.

[9]

Holding Together the Backchannel Experience

By following the examples of good speakers, you, too, can engage the backchannel successfully

C hris Brogan had never seen an audience quite like this one.

It was September 2009 and Chris was scheduled to speak during the final slot of the New Media Atlanta conference—an event for marketers who use social media in their work.

An expert on the topic of the conference, Chris gives about 100 presentations a year to technology-savvy audiences that have a backchannel.

When Chris sees people using Twitter as a backchannel, he generally finds them to be polite, in part, because people identify themselves in their public profiles. But today in Atlanta, members of the audience were using a backchannel tool called BackNoise that allows people to remain anonymous. And Chris saw that people were not being polite.

Others at the conference were noticing the same thing. Attendee Stacy Williams wrote in a blog post what was happening:

> As the second speaker started, people on BackNoise started bashing his PowerPoint slide design, and then his content. His content was pretty basic—I wasn't learning anything new—so I distracted myself by continuing to watch the conversation on BackNoise. It degenerated from bad to worse. As the day went on, there were some posts of substance, such as people saying that they wanted more "how to" information than they were getting... But most of the conversation deteriorated to personal attacks on the presenters... A majority of the comments were just plain mean in an irrelevant way—not constructive criticism, but rude, boorish, even vicious remarks.

The backchannel comments were *snarky*—a social media term combining the words *snide* and *remark,* most often referring to sarcastic comments users make online.

And Chris would soon be taking the stage in front of this very snarky backchannel.

As the time for his presentation neared, Chris remembers thinking to himself, "What am I going to do?"

Turning Around an Unruly Backchannel

In his role as an advisor to companies on how to engage social media, Chris preaches the gospel that it is essential to listen to what people are saying when they use tools like blogs, Twitter, and a backchannel. So he had been all ears since he arrived in Atlanta the night before. He approached people at dinner or during breaks and asked them what was on their minds and what they were interested in learning.

As the conference proceeded the next morning, Chris was very aware of what was happening in the backchannel. Beyond the snarky comments, he also saw another side to the situation—people in the audience were voicing concerns and frustrations. And he thought many of the comments carried a nugget of truth—some of the presentations were indeed too high level or not centered on the audience.

So Chris decided he needed to do something unconventional to turn the situation—and the backchannel—around.

> **tip** ❭ Watch the full video of Chris's presentation at New Media Atlanta on his blog at www.chrisbrogan.com/what-i-told-them-at-new-media-atlanta/. (Recorded by Run Level Media – Atlanta)

Chris walked up to the stage where there was no podium standing between him and his audience. In his hand was a piece of paper with 15 points he wanted to make during his presentation. He had no PowerPoint slides to show the audience. Instead, he made a bold move and chose to display the BackNoise backchannel on the screen behind him (**Figure 9-1**).

FIGURE 9-1:
In the video recording of his presentation, Chris Brogan displays the backchannel to defuse its snarky tone at the New Media Atlanta conference in September 2009.

Then he began his presentation.

Chris says he could have gone on stage and said, "I'm Chris and here's why I'm important, with boring slides behind me." But instead Chris began his presentation by rapping a few lines of the Jay-Z song "Dirt Off Your Shoulder":

> *All the ladies they love me, from the bleachers they screamin'*
> *All the ballers is bouncin' they like the way I be leanin'*
> *All the rappers be hatin', off the track that I'm makin'*
> *But all the hustlers they love it just to see one of us make it*

His aim with the lyrics came in the last line—he wanted his audience to know that he was one of them—and he succeeded as the audience roared in laughter and showed their approval.

Then he said, "Can we all just stand up for a minute, please—get your body up just for a minute. God we've been standing still!" People applauded as they stood up, feeling some physical relief to the tension that had been building up over the day.

As he pointed to BackNoise on the screen, he asked, "What part of social media is sitting perfectly still and snarking?" The audience replied with laughter.

By pointing to the screen Chris spoke directly to the elephant in the room—the outsized influence the snarky backchannel had been having on the event.

Still pointing at the screen he said, "Always confront the things you're afraid of head-on!" The audience applauded.

Chris asked the audience to sit down as he continued, "The most important part of social media is listening. I listened all day to this," as he pointed to the backchannel onscreen and people voiced their approval. "I wanted to see what it was about, because there is always truth in snark. The only thing wrong is that negative doesn't tell you how to fix it." Chris made his remarks in a playful tone, and people laughed as he continued, "Quit your bitching! Come up with the next conference! Because that's what's missing."

> **tip ❯** To continue learning about how to engage the backchannel, watch video recordings of presentations where there is a backchannel and observe what speakers do well, and how they can improve. Visit www.backchannelbook.com for links to videos and discussions about engaging the backchannel.

Chris had confronted the backchannel commenters head-on, addressing the negativity and holding them accountable for what they had been writing. But he did this in a friendly way that addressed them as if he were talking to them one-on-one. "But that's OK because you got the sound out of your voice," he said. "I recognize that you're there; that you're a person."

Chris looked at the backchannel screen where the comments were still being made. He called out a positive comment and thanked the person who wrote it.

Then he addressed what he thought to be a root cause of the snarky feedback. "The problem with marketing...is it is all bullhorn," he said. "It's all 'you the audience, me the stage.'" He described an Open Space–inspired event he co-founded that took the stage away. "PodCamp is an event where we all sit side by side," he said. "You can't snark because *you* are the content. The reason we did that was for that," as he pointed to the screen. "Because we all don't have the answer—we *all* have the answer."

Referring to comments in the backchannel about people wanting more practical tips, Chris asked, "Who all wanted 'how-to'?" as he launched into a series of examples of what people can do with social media.

At the end of his hour-long presentation, Chris received sustained applause from the audience, and later glowing reviews from bloggers.

What could have been a major backchannel explosion or a negative exchange Chris had managed to defuse in the first three minutes of his talk.

This example of how Chris engaged the backchannel ties together many of the threads in this book, as he managed to hold together the fast-moving, free-form, and sometimes rambunctious backchannel experience.

The 10-point checklist to managing an unruly backchannel

The previous example offers a 10-point checklist of what you can do to engage the backchannel:

1. Establish a reputation.
2. Listen and collect stories.
3. Dispense with pretense.
4. Talk to the elephant in the room (if there is one).
5. Make it you, you, you instead of me, me, me.

6. Check in with the audience early and often.

7. Improvise.

8. Stay grounded.

9. Ignore the small stuff.

10. Keep things in perspective.

Chris is living proof that it's possible to not just survive, but to thrive in the new world of the backchannel.

And it's something you can do, too, by following the checklist as follows.

Establish a Reputation

Something that's not obvious in watching the video of Chris's presentation is that he had worked hard well in advance to establish a reputation as someone the audience could trust.

Chris is a prolific writer in his blog, newsletter, website, and on Twitter (he has written more than 50,000 tweets and has more than 100,000 followers). He wrote a *New York Times* bestseller and seeks out speaking engagements to spread his message about effective ways to use social media.

When Chris walked on the stage, audience members already knew who he was even if they hadn't met him, and they looked forward to what he had to say.

Like Chris, some of the ways you can establish your reputation include

- Becoming a trusted expert in your field.
- Maintaining a current and relevant website.
- Starting a blog and posting regularly.
- Tweeting regularly and growing your list of followers.
- Seeking out speaking engagements.
- Writing articles and e-books.
- Volunteering to be a guest writer on other blogs.
- Writing a book for a major publisher.
- Helping others to become better at what they do.

There are many good books on how to establish and maintain a good reputation using social media tools, including Chris's new book, *Trust Agents* (Wiley, 2009), written with Julien Smith. Search your online bookseller for the term "social media" and you'll find the latest books on the topic. Although some of the books are geared toward businesses, most of the principles apply equally to developing your reputation as a speaker.

Listen and Collect Stories

As Chris described in his presentation, he had spent the day listening to what was happening. According to Chris, "There are always times (as a speaker) where you have to come and go (to an event), but if ever you can take the extra time to get to know the audience ahead of time, to commune amongst them ahead of the speech, they feel like they know you. The isolation approach is not the way to go."

Instead, Chris recommends you spend as much time as possible getting to know your audience, especially by circulating among people during breaks between sessions.

The key to getting to know them, according to Chris, is "Ask people about themselves." If people know who you are, they may ask you to talk about yourself, but according to Chris, you need to turn around the situation quickly so that you get people to talk about themselves and the challenges they face.

Chris describes that part of the value of asking questions and listening is that you get stories from people that you can use in your presentation. He remembers hearing a story during a coffee break about bloggers who knew of a restaurant in danger of losing financing. The bloggers rallied and created a social media campaign to show the bank the restaurant had living, breathing fans, and saved the restaurant. Chris now includes the anecdote in presentations as an example of the power of social media.

CeCe Salomon-Lee agrees, writing in a blog comment, "Before social media, I advised my clients to attend the conference and chat with people about which presentations were captivating and what trends were impacting them directly. This way, my client can then infuse their presentations with these anecdotes. What this did was...personalize the speaker to the audience because he/she...was paying attention to the content at the conference and...wasn't just walking in an hour before his/her presentation and leaving afterward."

> **tip ⟩** See Chapter 7 for more practical ways to research your audience and collect audience anecdotes you can integrate into your presentation.

Dispense with Pretense

At the start of every presentation, Chris aims to establish a level playing field with his audience. "I want them thinking 'this guy is like me,'" he says.

"I try to front-load my presentations with as much humility and self-deprecating humor as possible." Chris says, "I'm trying to dispel fears that I'm full of myself or that I'm arrogant."

He feels he needs to do this because, "There's a huge abundance of arrogance out there—(with speakers who) think the reason they have the stage is because 'you've put me in power.'" Or, speakers may be self-conscious or nervous and create a wall between themselves and their audiences, which can come across as arrogance. But Chris says, "Speakers fail if they lose connectivity with their audience. I don't leave a room unless I have 100 new friends."

Chris is able to keep the presentation experience very human, natural, and down to earth. He uses a conversational tone, and tells stories about people who are facing real problems, and how they engaged them.

"I am really preaching the gospel of being human," Chris says. "The speakers I'm enamored with are reaching into the depth of humanity. They're a person."

Talk to the Elephant in the Room (If There Is One)

In most of his presentations, Chris immediately sets a warm and accessible tone by throwing out a welcome mat to the backchannel, inviting people to have their laptops, smart phones, and Twitter open during his presentation. He tells his audience upfront that they should apply the Law of Two Feet and leave his talk and go to another speaker's presentation, though few take him up on his offer—the very act of inviting people to leave makes them want to stay even more.

But in Atlanta, the backchannel had actually become a significant force at the event itself. Chris decided to address the backchannel right away when he showed it on the stage.

As you learned in Chapter 6, displaying a backchannel onscreen can distract an audience because it visually dominates the room, and the comments are often off-topic and snarky. But his need to display the backchannel overruled the distraction it created because he needed to

- Acknowledge the impact the backchannel had made that day.

- Make the backchannel public to encourage self-regulation.

- Neutralize the negativity.

- Use the same medium the backchannel had been using.

If you face a negative backchannel or any other topic that nobody is talking about, bring it up right away so you can engage and overcome it.

Make It You, You, You Instead of Me, Me, Me

As Chris was listening to the backchannel feedback that day, he heard "a couple of complaints (that the content of some presentations was all about) me, me, me. So I started out you, you, you."

He centered his material on the audience by first bringing up the situation with the backchannel because it was on everyone's mind. Then he launched into a mix of top-level insight, interesting case studies, and practical takeaways that his audiences can apply when they leave the room.

A number of things you did in earlier chapters make sure you keep the presentation focused on the audience instead of you:

- Completing the Four Tweets worksheet (Chapter 6) makes sure you look at things from your audience's perspective.

- Using a story structure (Chapter 6) makes sure you orient the entire presentation around a challenge your audience faces.

- Conducting audience research (Chapter 7) helps you find stories and examples you can include in your presentation.

- Involving your audience (Chapter 7) allows them to contribute their thoughts and ideas.

Speaker Sacha Chua writes in her blog that presenting is "not about advertising your company. It's not about building your reputation. It's about helping people learn something, understand something, or be inspired to do something. It's about starting a hundred or a thousand conversations. It's about discovery."

Check In with the Audience Early and Often

Central to holding together the backchannel experience is tone—the spirit and mood of the gathering that you set. Author and speaker Steven Berlin Johnson describes that when he gets up on a stage,

> The primary thing I'm thinking about—more than the words themselves, most of which I've said before in roughly the same sequence—is the room tone. Is the audience with me or against me? Are they having fun? Are they confused? Am I talking at too technical a level? Am I being condescending and talking down?

Chris agrees with the need to check on the tone with your audience, as he writes in his blog:

> Make sure that you check in, frequently with your audience. Be sure they're moving along with your presentation. If you see eyes glazing, react (either by livening up your speaking tone, or by noting where people start to glaze and fixing it in a subsequent effort). If you see enthusiasm, look at that person for inspiration. But always check in. Often.

Several times during his Atlanta presentation, Chris looked over at the backchannel screen and asked, "How am I doing, does everybody hate me?" or "Are they killing me?" Then he looked at the screen and commented, "All right. Good enough."

In a CNET News article by Daniel Terdiman titled "How to survive the next-gen confab," blogger Robert Scoble describes how speakers can be more responsive to audiences:

> Part of it is just having audience empathy, understanding what the audience is thinking about you, looking into their eyes and gauging their reactions. And if it goes south, not arguing with them. Because you can deconstruct it later. At that moment, your role is as a representative of the audience. You have to put yourself in their shoes right then and there.

But as Chris demonstrated at New Media Atlanta, that doesn't mean you have to be passive and let the audience control or dominate you. In his opening remarks, Chris directly confronted the audience over their snarky comments. He used a friendly tone as he let them know that he was listening to them and that there was some truth to their criticism, but at the same time he let them know they needed to do more than complain—they needed to come up with a solution.

Later in his presentation, Chris typed directly into the BackNoise interface displayed on the screen, making a comment about his audience being too quiet. This act of directly and visibly contributing to the backchannel on the screen demonstrated to the audience that he was right there in the chat room with them. They now knew that what had been a conversation apart from the speakers that day was now front and center of his and everyone else's attention.

Improvise

Part of the secret to Chris's success at presentations is his ability to quickly adjust to changing situations. Consultant Jen McClure describes Chris as speaking really fast, being funny and in the moment. "He's quick and quick-witted, and you kind of have to be there. He's so speaky, and off the cuff."

You never know what to expect when you're in a presentation with a backchannel, so it's important to develop your skills at improvising.

Applying the "Yes, and…" technique from comedy improv

At the famous Groundlings comedy improvisation school in Los Angeles, the central premise is to always add new information to keep the action moving. After performers listen to what someone has said, they begin their sentences with "Yes, and…", then continue their improvised statements from that point.

According to the rules of the Groundlings, you don't say the word "no," which would put a jarring halt to the flow of the story and diminish the options for creative responses. You also don't argue, because improvisation needs new information to keep going, and arguing would be pointless. This affirmative orientation of the improvised statements keeps the positive energy going through the course of dialogue, and keeps the pathway open for a continuous flow of energy.

As you listen to comments or engage new topics during a presentation, begin by using the phrase, "yes, and…" and then completing the rest of the sentence. As you complete the thought, relate the previous topic to the new. For example, if a comment in the backchannel says, "That example doesn't apply to me," you might call out the comment and say, "Yes, and the way you can apply this example to any situation is to look at the underlying principles…"

One of the most entertaining dimensions of comedy improv is when a performer somehow links previous unrelated information to a new topic. As you can do this with your own topics, you'll find your audience engaged and interested, surprised to see how you will cleverly make the transition between unrelated topics.

By applying the rule of "yes, and…" to your own responses to audience members, you also maintain a positive tone and keep the story moving forward. And as you're conscious to avoid saying "no" or arguing with your audience members, you can be sure to keep a positive flow of information moving forward from beginning to end.

Using no slides

Although sometimes he uses PowerPoint for presentations, in Atlanta Chris decided to use no slides at all—instead he had only a piece of paper in his hand so he could have more flexibility to respond to the situation he faced.

"Slides lock me into a story line," Chris says. "If I have paper, I can be a magician." As Chris watches the dynamics of the audience he adjusts his material accordingly. For example, "If they seem interested in case studies, I can be more of a storyteller" by giving examples of his ideas in action.

Leaving space to be dynamic

Chris recommends speakers "Put air in the speech so you can change things, should the circumstance arise that you need to be dynamic."

Chapters 6 and 7 described how you can create a simple structure around a few important ideas you want to convey. By letting go of the idea that you have to show your audience every step of the way—and instead providing a structure and letting them fill in the blanks—you open up more conversational space and improve your audience's experience.

When you allow space for yourself to be more adaptable—within an established structure, of course—you'll be dealing with comments and material that may not always segue smoothly from one topic to the next. Keep things flowing smoothly throughout your presentation by mastering transitions.

As Chris demonstrates during his talks, you really have to think quickly on your feet as you respond to changing circumstances, and the most readily available tools you have to move smoothly through the change are your wit and your voice.

tip 〉 If you're particularly adventurous, try presenting a completely Twitter-led presentation. Esther Lim wrote about seeing a session like this that was "driven by what the audience wanted to talk about. Less a presentation more of a mass dialog." She lists the benefits as being "highly engaging and energetic" and "memorable," but the drawback being that it "has huge potential to lose focus and become chaotic—(it) requires the speaker to really know the subject matter and have the composure to respond quickly."

Stay Grounded

In the past, you may have thought you needed to gain control of every detail of the presentation experience in order to be successful. There's no getting around the fact that with a backchannel you have more to do, more to know about, and more to be aware of. The goal then is to let go of the idea that you need to fully control everything; there's no way to control what your audience thinks and does even if you wanted to. Instead, stay grounded in the confidence in your material and your passion for your topic.

Being confident and at ease with your material

Knowing your framework and your material is essential to gain the confidence and ease you need to be able to really listen to your audience and respond to changing circumstances.

According to Nancy White:

> If I as presenter am focused on "delivery" I'm not in listening mode. All the "audience" theoretically are. So they are more prepared for integrating and responding than the presenter in performance mode. Perhaps if we were better prepared, more at ease, and confident as performer, we'd be able to more easily move away from performer to listener and conversational participant.

Uncertainty in your topic or fear that you'll make a mistake are the biggest obstacles to finding the state of ease you need to move with the flow of the presentation experience. The point at which you are able to deliver the core material you have to present without the aid of any tools is generally the point at which you are confident enough to move into the zone where you can fully be present and adaptable to your audience.

Loving your topic and loving to talk about it

As Chris demonstrates in his presentations, the love of your topic is the core of what will make you more effective as a presenter in any context. Audiences are more than willing to overlook flaws in public speaking skills if they detect that you're authentically passionate about your material.

Standing up in front of an audience should be an exhilarating experience, where you learn something new each time you do it.

It's also an opportunity to be yourself, which is especially important to the backchannel—they will be the first to point out that you're not.

Ignore the Small Stuff

Throughout Chris's presentation in Atlanta, some people in the backchannel continued to post trivial comments on the screen, or just typed things to draw attention to themselves. Chris ignored the off-topic comments, and instead focused on the ones that applied to the material he was describing.

If you call out the trivial, you give the trivial status it doesn't deserve. By ignoring what is not important, you don't let the backchannel take control.

Keep Things in Perspective

By all means, you don't have to let the backchannel take over your presentation life. You do need to embrace the change and do the necessary preparation and planning. But once you have the important pieces in place, you can let go and focus wholly on delivering a great experience.

Jen McClure says, "As a presenter, I just try to forget it," explaining that paying too much attention to the backchannel can take you off your game if you let it.

Jared Spool agrees, saying "If it's freaking you out, ignore it."

Especially if you're feeling nervous about engaging the backchannel, Chris says, "It's the kind of thing you can ignore. You don't have to jump in on it." If you're already overwhelmed with preparing for a presentation and the thought of public speaking, "It could be a terrible thing to add to your plate."

If you're feeling overwhelmed, take the backchannel one step at a time.

During your first experience with a backchannel, ignore it during the presentation. But afterward, review the Twitterstream to see what people said and take their thoughts into account as you adjust your material.

The next time you give a presentation, add your Twitter credentials to your title slide and welcome the backchannel. And the time after that, take your first Twitter break to see how it goes for you.

Engage the backchannel at the pace that's appropriate for you, and keep in mind the positive possibilities that this new conversation is something that will continually make you a better speaker.

Backchannel to the Future

So what does the future hold for the backchannel?

The wave of new social technologies has upended industry after industry, including music, television, publishing, and journalism. It was only a matter of time before change entered the meeting room.

And now we stand at a watershed moment in presentation history.

The past century has introduced breathtaking change not seen since the foundation of oratory by the Greeks, including the influence of radio and television; the introduction of microphones, projectors, and presentation software into the meeting room; and now the arrival of the Internet-ready backchannel.

This change is different, because where the other technologies amplified the Greek model for oratory, the backchannel may actually turn it upside down.

For a very long time, the world has centered on presenters. But now, the world is re-centering around audience members. Putting someone on a pedestal—or a lectern—has always come at a cost, because to make someone higher is to make someone lesser.

The backchannel dismantles the pedestal, and gives everyone equal access to the same information. As the power balance is leveled, the skill set of presenters fundamentally changes, and shifts more toward gifts of navigation, facilitation, and inspiration.

The traditional lecture format, bullet point slides, and post-presentation Q&A session are becoming dinosaurs in this fast-moving world. Each of these social tools has offered some efficiency or benefit that was appropriate for the time, but times are radically changing, and it is time for these methods to evolve into new ones that are a better fit for our needs.

The rise of the backchannel is nothing to fear; rather it is something to embrace. A presentation has always been about the audience anyway, and if the audience wants to join in and shape an experience, presenters should be happy for it.

Instead of being in a confined space of 100 people in a room, with a backchannel we are suddenly 10,000. And what can 10,000 people do who are passionate, connected, and working together?

The backchannel is about people—people who gather together in person to share a common vision, move in the same direction, and get something done.

Only time will tell what the future of presentations will become, but in the meantime, be sure to keep your eyes on the backchannel.

Appendixes

[Appendix A]

The Four Tweets Worksheet

As you learned in Chapter 6, the Four Tweets worksheet is built from a Twitter search results page and features space to write four results.

The challenge is for you to draft the four most important ideas from your presentation that you would like your audience members to tweet to their followers.

In tweet 1 write the single summary tweet (in 140 characters or less, of course) that you would like your audience members to tweet to their followers to summarize your presentation.

In tweets 2 through 4, write your three supporting tweets that explain your summary.

twitter | Search |

Realtime results for   0.09 seconds

The Ten Tweets Worksheet

Like the Four Tweets worksheet in Appendix A, the Ten Tweets worksheet on the next page is built from a Twitter search results page, except it features space to write ten results.

In tweet 1, write the single summary tweet that best summarizes your entire presentation.

In tweets 2 through 4, write the three supporting tweets that explain your summary tweet.

In tweets 5 and 6, write down the links to the two most useful resources from your presentation that you'd like your audience to pass on to other people.

In tweets 7 and 8, sketch the two slides you'd like your audience to photograph and tweet to their followers.

In tweets 9 and 10, write two tweets that describe how you would like your audience to describe your delivery.

twitter [   ] [Search]

Realtime results for   0.09 seconds

[ ]

[ ]

[ ]

[ ]

[ ]

[ ]

[ ]

[ ]

[ ]

[ ]

INDEX

A

A Seat Apart, 155, 156
account setup (Twitter), 36–37
active knowledge, 168–169
age, of Twitter users, 31
Alley, Michael, 137
American Idol (TV show), 30
American Society of Association Executives (ASAE), 188
anger at presentations, 189
archiving presentation materials, 107
ASAE (American Society of Association Executives), 188
Atkinson, Cliff, *Beyond Bullet Points,* 124, 129, 172
attendees list, on presentation home pages, 104
audiences. *See also* presenters
    changes in, 77–80
    checking in with, 202
    code of conduct for backchannel use, 86
    communications within, 53
    distractions for, 71–72
    expanding, using Twitter, 51, 54
    improved relationship with, 63–64
    information sharing within, 60–61
    needs versus wants of, 93
    polling of, 167
    presentations, increased expectations for, 77–79
    presentations, involvement in (*See* network conversations)
    presenters, relationship with, 24–26, 62–63, 94–95
    presenters' researching about, 151–152
    presenters' understanding of, 199
    reaching out to, 92
    size of, 17–18
    Twitter's, 31
    using the backchannel, photo of, 90
auto tweeting, 165–166

B

backchannel agreements, new, 86
backchannel conversation, joining. *See* network conversations
Backchannel Golden Rule, 157–158
backchannel(s). *See also* audiences; blowups; instant feedback, handling; presenters; Twitter
    constructive versus destructive use of, 18–19
    definition, 17
    disproportional influence, 74
    engaging (*See* network conversations)
    future of, 207–208
    importance of monitoring, 22
    live display of, 109
    preparing for (*See* preparing for the backchannel)
    research on, 31
    risks and rewards of (*See* rewards of backchannel; risks of backchannel)
    unofficial, 33
background color, on presentation slides, 138

BackNoise, 34, 194, 195, 203

bar charts, human, 170–171

BarCamp, 84

Basen, Ira, 72–73

BBP Story Template, 129

Beyond Bullet Points (Atkinson), 124, 129, 172

big story, of presentations, 96, 97–98

Blog to Book. See From Blog to Book Deal
    (SXSW panel session)

BloggerCon, 85

blogs, books versus, 10

blowups. *See also* instant feedback,
    handling
    at *From Blog to Book Deal* panel, 14–16,
        19–21
    at Canadian Institute Conference on
        Social Media, 72–73
    effects of, 76
    at Les Blogs conference, 68–70
    negative comments and, 184
    preventing, 86
    at SXSW conference, 74–75

books, blogs versus, 10

boring material, 189

brainstorming presentation ideas, 126–127

broadcast media, Twitter as, 44

Brogan, Chris
    audience-centric approach, 201
    audience check-ins, 202
    on audiences, understanding, 199
    on dynamic nature of presentations, 204
    elephant in the room and, 200–201
    on presentations, 121
    presentations without slides, 204
    on pretense, 200
    reputation of, 198
    snarkiness, confronting, 194–197,
        202–203
    Trust Agents, 199

buy-in, for presentations, 159–160

C

Call to Action slide, 129

calling out negative comments, 183–186

camera phones, presentation slides and,
    141–142

camps, 83–84

Canadian Institute Conference on Social
    Media, 72–73

case studies, collecting, 153–154

celebrities, use of Twitter by, 31

CEOs, use of Twitter by, 31

change, embracing, 86

chaos, as backchannel risk, 74–76

character counts, tools for, 134

chat rooms
    as backchannel, 34
    password-protected, 54
    for presentation home pages, 106

Chatango, 34

ChatMaker, 34

Chatzy, 34

checklist for managing unruly backchannel,
    197–207

Chua, Sacha, 181, 201

Cluetrain Manifesto (Levine et al.), 25

code of conduct for backchannel use,
    86. *See also* Golden Rule of the
    Backchannel

Cold Spring Harbor Biology of Genomes
    meeting, 71

commenting on information, 59

computerese, backchannel in, 17

comScore, 30, 31

concerts, tweeting at, 30

conferences (events). *See also* audiences;
    presentations; presenters
    hashtags for, 8, 111
    registration for, and online surveys, 153
    use of backchannel at, 2–27
    use of Twitter at, 32–33

Congress, use of Twitter by, 31

context, lack of, in backchannel, 70

conversational presentations, 149–150

conversational zones, 169–170

conversations. *See also* network
    conversations
    presentations versus, 78–79, 147–149
    privacy of online versus offline, 70

Corrigan, Eileen, 22–23

Cowan, Nelson, 117

criteria for choosing tools, 36

Cut & Paste Character Count tool, 134

Cuthrell, Jay, 126

D

demographics of Twitter users, 31

dialogs, using the backchannel, 59–62. *See
    also* network conversations

Dimdim, 106

diplomacy, backchannel in, 17

distraction, as backchannel risk, 71–72

document sharing, 34

Donella Evoniuk, 83

Duarte, Nancy, 140

Dyson, Esther, 187

E

EduCamp, 84

educators, use of Twitter by, 31

Edventure Holdings, 187

elephant in the room, 200–201

Elliott, Timo, 166

email, 97, 154

embedded live video feeds, on presentation
    home pages, 105–106

embedded videos, on presentation home
    page, 104

enhancing information, 58

Escape from Cubicle Nation (Pam Slim
    blog), 4

EtherPad, 34

events (conferences). *See also* audiences;
    presentations; presenters
    hashtags for, 8, 111
    registration for, and online surveys, 153
    use of backchannel at, 2–27
    use of Twitter at, 32–33

external audiences for presentations, 54

F

face-to-face meetings, 61, 154

facilitators, presenters as, 150

feedback. *See also* instant feedback,
    handling
    increasing, 62–63

feedback scenarios, 186–190

filters, presenters as, 117–118

Find People page (Twitter), 45

Flickr, 6, 23, 111

followers (on Twitter)
    as additional audience members, 54
    attracting, 95
    inviting, 45–46
    numbers of, 44

following (subscribing to) Twitter posts, 5,
    44–46

Forrest, Hugh, 178, 179

Fost, Dan, 74–75

four tweets, rule of, 118–121

Fraser, Jaine, 178

From Blog to Book Deal (SXSW panel
    session)
    Kawasaki-Hess interaction at, 14–15,
        19–21
    live-Twittering of, 2–27
    participants, photo of, 6
    post-sessions comments on, 22–24

G

Gillmor, Dan, 25, 187
glossary on backchannel feedback, 185
Godin, Seth, 11
Golden Rule of the Backchannel, 157–158
Google Docs, 34
graphics, adding to presentation slides, 139–140
Gray, Dave, 16
Groundlings comedy improvisation school, 203

H

Hamlin, Kaliya, 85
handouts, online availability, 104
Harvard Business School, 44
hashtags
    adding to tweets, 39
    for conferences, 32–33
    example of, 8
    multiple, monitoring, 42–43
    negative, 185
    promoting, 111
headlines, for presentation slides, 137
Hello application, 155, 156
Hess, Whitney
    benefits of tweeting for, 10
    on Kawasaki, 14
    Kawasaki, interaction with, 15, 19–21
    live-Twittering *From Blog to Book Deal*, 2–3, 4–14
    reputation, 7
    as Twitterer, 2
hiccups, cure for, as Twitter demonstration, 50–51, 55–56
hierarchy, presentation preparation and, 128–134
Hokanson, Kristin, 83

home pages for presentations
    about, 99–100
    archiving materials for, 107
    attendees list, 104
    backchannel tools on, 106–107
    embedded live video feeds, 105–106
    embedded videos, 104
    information pyramid and, 132–133
    online handouts, 104
    pre-presentation uses for, 152
    source materials on, 168
human bar charts, 170–171
human memory, 117, 128–129
Hurt, Jeff, 77, 163

I

identity (on Twitter), establishing, 38–39
ignoring negative comments, 183
improvisation
    by presenters, 203–205
    visual, 171–172
in-person meetings, 61, 154
incivility, risk of, 68–70
information
    efficient ways of sending, 90–91
    engagement with, 57–59
    multiple sources for, 77
    new, brain's limited capacity for processing, 117
information hierarchies, 128–130
information overload, avoiding, 129
instant feedback, handling, 178–190
    checklist for managing unruly backchannel, 197–207
    feedback scenarios, practicing, 186–190
    glossary, 185
    negative feedback, neutralizing, 179–181
    negative feedback, power of, 178–179
    negative feedback, preparing for, 181–182

negative feedback, responses to, 182–186

non-anonymous feedback tools, 180

Internet Relay Chat (IRC), 17, 31, 34, 68

interpersonal relationships, 59–62

intra-audience conversations, 52–53

iPhone, TweetDeck for, 43

IRC (Internet Relay Chat), 17, 31, 34, 68

is.gd (URL shortener service), 7

iStockphoto.com, 139

J

Japan, text messaging at concerts, 30

Johnson, Steven Berlin, 75, 202

K

Kawasaki, Guy
    on agents, 12
    on book proposals, 13
    on books versus blogs, 10
    Corrigan and, 23
    Hess, interaction with, 15, 19–21
    Hess's tweets on, 14–15
    Twitter user name, 6

Key Point slides, 129

Keynote presentation tool, 136

Keynote Tweet, 166

Kim, Peter, 152

Klein, Stephanie, 6, 10, 11, 12

Kleon, Austin, 23

L

Lacy, Sarah, 74–75

LaidOffCamp, 84

Law of Two Feet (Law of Mobility), 82, 157, 200

Lawson, Karen, 161, 168–169

Le Meur, Loïc, 25

Lee, Kate, 6, 12

Les Blogs conference, 68–69

Li, Charlene, 152

Lim, Esther, 205

linguistics, backchannel in, 17

links
    in presentation's four tweets, 133
    in tweets, 7

live display of backchannel, 109

live-Twittering
    description of, 4
    effects of, 22
    facilitating, 108–109
    permission for, 71

live video streaming, 143

Livestream, 105, 143

M

MacLeod, Hugh, 10, 11, 12, 13

marketing, using Twitter, 46

Mayer, Richard E., 122

McClure, Jen, 25, 135, 203, 206

Meebo, 34

memory, human, 117, 128–129

Metaphorically Selling (Miller), 126

metaphors, for presentations, 125–126

Metcalfe, Ben, 69–70

microphones, use during presentations, 164

Miller, Anne, 126

Milstein, Sarah, 46

mind mapping, 126–127

Minnesota Public Radio, 186

Minnesota Society of Professional Journalists, 186

Minto, Barbara, 131

The Minto Pyramid Principle: Logic in Writing, Thinking and Problem Solving (Minto), 131 misinformation, 187

Mitchell, Olivia
    on buy-in, methods of obtaining, 160
    on negative comments, 183
    on re-tweeting questions, 163
    on reaching non-Twitter audiences, 154
    on Twitterstream, displaying, 110

mobile devices, accessing Twitter on, 43

Mobility, Law of (Law of Two Feet), 82,
    157, 200

moderators (for presentations), 22, 162–163

Morgan, Nick, 169–170

multiple platforms for presentations,
    97–107

multiple Twitterstreams, monitoring, 42–43

N

Nacchio, Joe, 187

National Educational Computing
    Conference (NECC), 40–41, 82–83,
    106–107

Nature (journal), 71

negative feedback
    neutralizing, 179–181
    power of, 178–179
    preparing for, 181–182
    responses to, 182–186
    scenarios for, 186–190
    snarkiness, dealing with, 194–197
    snowballing of, 75–76

negotiations, use of backchannel in, 30

network conversations, 146–175
    audience engagement during, 166–172
    audience polling, 167
    automating backchannel involvement,
        165–166
    backchannel as, 56–57
    backchannel display during Twitter
        breaks, 164

    backchannel setup, pre-presentation,
        154–156
    continuing, 174–175
    conversational presentations and,
        149–150
    conversational zones, 169–170
    creating, 146–149
    human bar charts, 170–171
    presentation-conversation hybrid,
        creating, 146–149
    presentation wrap-up, 172
    starting the conversation, 151–154
    strong presentation start, importance of,
        158–161
    Twitter, integrating into PowerPoint, 166
    Twitter breaks, 161–165
    Twitterstream checks, post-
        presentation, 173–174
    visual improvisation, 171–172
    welcoming the backchannel, 156–158

New Media Atlanta conference, 194–197

O

one-to-many presentations, 52

online surveys, 152–153

Open Space Technology, 80–85

Open Space Technology: A User's Guide
    (Owen), 80

O'Reilly, Tim, 46

organizational charts, 128

Owen, Harrison, 80

Owyang, Jeremiah, 152

P

panel moderators, 22

participation, audience desire for, 78–79

PBworks.com (collaborative tools website),
    101–102

PC Forum, 187
Pew Internet & American Life Project, 31–32
pictures, adding to Twitter profile, 38
PodCamp, 84, 197
Pogue, David, 50–51, 55–56
Pogue's Post (blog), 50
Poll Everywhere, 110
polling audiences, 167
PowerPoint, 135–136, 166
preparing for the backchannel, 90–113
    attracting Twitter followers, 95
    audiences, assumptions about, 91–92
    learning new skills, 92
    long-term audience relationship,
        94–95
    multiple presentation platforms,
        97–107
    writing once, publishing many, 97–98
presentation-conversation hybrids. *See*
    network conversations
Presentation Zen (Reynolds), 140
presentations. *See also* network
    conversations; Twitter-friendly
    presentations
    archiving material from, 107
    audience expectations for, 77–79
    audience involvement in (*See* network
        conversations)
    backchannel's disconnection from,
        99–100
    backchannel's influence on, 51–57
    big story of, 96, 97–98
    constants in, 90–91
    conversational, 149–150
    conversations versus, 78–79, 147–149
    facilitating backchannel for, 108–110
    focus of, 91
    home pages for (*See* home pages for
        presentations)
    improving, using Twitterstream, 51

    involving audience in, 160–161
    key areas of, 93
    live video feeds, 105–106
    moderators for, 162–163
    as one-time events, 94
    one-to-many, 52
    possible outcomes for, 122
    preparing online, 100–101
    single-word slides, 160
    slideless, 204
    software for, 135–136
    strong start, importance of, 158–161
    summary of changes impacting, 86
    Twitter reporters for, 108–109
    wikis and, 101–102
    writing once, publishing many, 97–98
presenters. *See also* audiences; preparing
    for the backchannel
    audience, knowledge of, 63–64
    audience, relationship with, 24–26,
        94–95
    audience research, 151–152
    audiences, understanding of, 199
    backchannel information, obtaining,
        55–56
    characteristics of good, 90
    distractions for, 71–72
    engagement with backchannel, 26
    as facilitators, 150
    as filters, 117–118
    network conversations and, 57
    Twitter as marketing tool for, 46
    Twitter monitoring by, 15
    use of tweets, 112
    walking into audience, 169–170
pretense, 200
privacy, of online versus offline
    conversations, 70
problem-solution structure, 124–125
ProductCamp, 84

Purewire, 44

pyramids, information hierarchies and, 130–134

Q

questions, tweeting of, 63

R

re-tweets (RT), 16, 60

refreshing Twitter search results page, 42

Reilly, Pete, 180

religious institutions, use of Twitter by, 31

reporting information, 58

reputation, establishing, 198–199

rewards of backchannel

    audience, improved relationship with, 63–64

    dialogs, expanded, 59–62

    feedback, increasing, 62–63

    information engagement, 57–59

    presentations and, 51–57

Reynolds, Garr, 140

risks of backchannel. *See also* instant feedback, handling

    chaos, 74–76

    distraction, 71–72

    incivility, 68–70

    unfairness, 72–74

RT (retweets), 16, 60

rule of four tweets, 118–121

S

Salomon-Lee, CeCe, 199

SavorChat, 34

Scandinavia, text messaging in, 30

scientific information, live-blogging of, 71

Scoble, Robert, 161, 202

Scott, David Meerman, 153, 170

searching, on Twitter, 40–42

Searls, Doc, 187

Seesmic Desktop, 43

Shandwick, Weber, 82

Sierra, Kathy, 127

Slideology (Duarte), 140

SlideRocket, 136

slides, preparing for presentations, 136–142

SlideShare, 57, 97

Slim, Pam

    blog by, 4

    as *Blog to Book* panel moderator, 2, 9, 12, 13, 15, 19–21

    Corrigan and, 23

    Twitter user name, 6

small stuff, ignoring, 206

Smith, Julien, 199

snark bomb, 185

snarkiness, dealing with, 194–197, 202–203

social hierarchies, 128

SocialOomph (formerly Tweetlater), 165

source citations, importance of, 101

source materials, 168

South by Southwest Interactive Festival. *See* SXSW

speakers. *See* presenters

Spool, Jared

    on human bar charts, 170–171

    on ignoring backchannel, 206

    on live displays of backchannel, 109

    on negative criticism, 182

    negative feedback, response to, 185

    Twitterstream, use of, 51

Stewart, David, 71

stories, collecting, 199

story structure for presentations

    four tweets and, 124–126

    hierarchy and, 129–130

    in presentation opening, 159

storyboards, 140–141

subscribing to (following) Twitter posts, 5, 44–46

SurveyMonkey, 153, 154

surveys, online, 152–153

Swan, Greg, 186, 187

SXSW (South by Southwest) Interactive Festival

    backchannel blowups at, 15, 19–21, 74–75, 187

    hashtag for, 8

    live-tweeting at, 2–3, 4–14

    photo of panel at, 6

Sysomos, 44

T

TechCrunch, 44

TED Conference, 98

television news, use of Twitter by, 31

ten tweets, 119, 211–212

Terdiman, Daniel, 202

Thornley, Joseph, 72–73

timeline (on Twitter), 36

Tinychat, 34, 35

Today's Meet, 34

tone, in online versus offline conversations, 70

tools for creating backchannels, 33–36

trivialities, ignoring, 206

Trott, Mena, 68–70

Trust Agents (Brogan), 199

tweckling, 185

TweetChat, 34

TweetDeck, 43

Tweetlater (SocialOomph), 165

tweets (Twitter posts)

    brevity, benefits of, 123

    character limit for, 7

    characteristics of good, 133

    components of, 4, 5–6, 7, 8

    description, 2

    emotional nature of, 14

    first, writing, 39

    public nature of, 5

    rule of four, 118–121

    website links in, 7

tweetups, 61

TwitPic, 57, 142

Twitter. *See also* followers (on Twitter); Twitter-friendly presentations

    accessing on mobile devices, 43

    account followers, numbers of, 44

    account setup, 36–37

    audience demographics, 31

    as backchannel tool, 33–34

    conferences, use at, 2–27

    first tweet, writing, 39

    home page, 30

    identity, establishing, 38–39

    monitoring multiple hashtags, 42–43

    popularity, 116

    rise of, 30–34

    searching, 40–42

    shortcomings, 35–36

    site visitors, numbers of, 30

    tweets, description of, 2

    user names, 5–6

    uses of, 3

The Twitter Book (O'Reilly and Milstein), 46

Twitter breaks, 161–165

Twitter communities

    growing, 44–46

Twitter-friendly presentations, 116–142

    audience-based focus of, 121, 122–123

    brainstorming ideas for, 126–127

    building sections of, 140–141

    camera phones and, 141–142

    distilling ideas for, 126–134

    four tweets, slides for, 134–135

Twitter-friendly presentations (continued)
  four tweets, worksheet for, 210
  hierarchy as tool for preparing, 128–134
  measuring success of, 123
  preparation for, using ten tweets, 120
  preparing slides for, 136–142
  presentation software for, 135–136
  presenter as filter, 117–118
  rule of four tweets and, 118–121, 133
  slide headings, 137
  story structure for preparing, 124–126
  ten tweets, worksheet for, 211–212
  video cameras and, 141–142
Twitter reporters, 108–109
Twitterers, evolution of, 61
twitterjacking, 76, 185
twitterlashing, 185
Twitterstreams
  archiving, 64, 174
  displaying, 42, 110
  multiple, monitoring, 42–43
  presentations and, 51
  previewing, 40–42
  reviewing with audience, 163
  Spool's use of, 51
  value of, 173–174
Two Feet, Law of (Law of Mobility), 82, 157, 200
Twtpoll, 167
TXTMob, 34

U

un-following Twitter posts, 7
unconferences, 85
unfairness, as backchannel risk, 72–74
unofficial backchannels, 33
URL shortener services, 7
user names (Twitter), 5–6
Ustream.tv, 105, 106, 107, 143

V

video cameras, presentation slides and, 141–142
video streaming, live, 143
visual improvisation, 171–172

W

We the Media (Gillmor), 187
Web 2.0 Expo, 152
web conferencing services, 106
Weber Shandwick (PR firm), 32
website addresses, URL shortener services for, 7
websites, as presentation channel, 97
"Welcome to Conference 2.0" (Fost), 74–75
White, Nancy, 56–57, 167, 182, 205
wikis, building presentations using, 101–102
Williams, Stacy, 194
wireless Internet connectivity, 108
WordCamp, 84
WordPress, 84
working memory, limitations of, 117
Working the Room (Morgan), 169
worksheets
  for four tweets, 119, 210
  for ten tweets, 211–212
writing once, publishing many, 97–98

Y

"yes, and" technique, 203–204
Young, Simon, 173
YouTube, 57, 97

Z

Zuckerberg, Mark, 74–75

twitter

Realtime results for   0.09 seconds

twitter

Search

Realtime results for

0.09 seconds

twitter

Search

Realtime results for   0.09 seconds